French
Academic Guide

Power-Glide French Academic Guide

Writers: Shauna Palmer, Gretchen Hilton
Editors: Geoff Groberg, Gretchen Hilton, Phillip Morris
Layout/Design: Erik D. Holley
Reviewers: Mary Graves, Soccorro Galusha-Luna, Mary Tanksley

French Academic Guide © 2001 Power-Glide. All rights reserved. No part of this publication may be reproduced, stored in a retrieval system or transmitted in any form or by any means, electronic, mechanical, photocopying, recording, scanning, or otherwise.
ISBN: 1-58204-068-0
PN 4607-01

POWER-GLIDE
FOREIGN LANGUAGE SCHOOL

Dear Language Learner,

Welcome to an incredible language learning experience. As you set out to learn your next language with Power-Glide, I can assure you that your diligence in applying yourself can result in a steady climb in your proficiency in the language, together with a considerable amount of pleasure along the way, and a growing love and appreciation of your new language.

As a human being, you are genetically adapted to learn a second language and even a third. But to learn any language efficiently and without great frustration you must proceed in nature's way.

Many have wrongly supposed that nature's way to learn a language is to approach it as tons of word and grammar memorization exercises to be endured, and that to score good grades a learner must get everything right from the first. They have made language study a long and tedious academic exercise, loaded with drills, always with imperfection viewed as the enemy. But if success were judged by the degree of fluency achieved by the great majority of learners who have endured the experience of language study in school settings, one would have to admit that teaching languages in schools has proved woefully unsuccessful. Even after years of such treatment, most students come away with little proficiency and a fear of speaking. The problem seems to be that the academic methods of analysis and drill, with native-like perfection the measuring stick, are very far from nature's way.

> *Dr. Blair, the creator of Power-Glide foreign language courses, invites you to learn a new language in a fun, motivational, rewarding, and natural way.*

There are commercial language courses that advertise: "Learn a language the way a child learns." What they in fact offer is nothing more than a tedious series of words, phrases, sentences and dialogs to hear, repeat and memorize. Some even provide background music, drum beats and sound effects to the torture. Scientific research into language acquisition clearly shows that that approach is a far cry from nature's way. It is as artificial, and as unsuccessful, as the analysis and drill methods traditionally used in schools and colleges.

Power-Glide language courses are designed to draw out the natural language-acquisition strategies of ordinary learners. The unique methodology of the courses has emerged through years of scientific study and teaching of language acquisition, decades of study of alternative approaches and hundreds of hours of experimentation with learners from kindergarten age to old age, and in more than a dozen languages. The courses are constantly in review, and are improved from year to year. Student response to the courses has been very positive, and parents, professional teachers and linguists have lavished praise on them.

You may be assured that you have in your hands a program that is changing the way the world conceives of language learning in the 21st century. Enjoy it. Let it empower you to speak and understand your next language, as it opens the door and allows you entry into another wonderful world.

Robert W. Blair, Ph.D.

Table of Contents

Overview 1
    Orientation 2
    Scope and Sequence 5
    Power-Glide Methodology 9

Sample Test 13

Lesson Plans 19
    French 1, Semester 1 21
        Section 1 21
        Section 2 25
        Section 3 28
    French 1, Semester 2 47
        Section 1 47
        Section 2 50
        Section 3 54
    French 2, Semester 1 71
        Section 1 71
        Section 2 74
        Section 3 76
    French 2, Semester 2 95
        Section 1 95
        Section 2 97
        Section 3 100

Overview

The information in this overview will:
- give you a brief orientation to the contents of this book
- instruct you on how to pursue credit
- outline the scope and sequence of course material
- explain Power-Glide methodology

Orientation

Scope and Sequence

The scope and sequence outlines the vocabulary content, grammar content, and objectives of the course. It is divided up into four semesters showing what content and grammar is taught in each. New content and grammar principles are introduced each semester and may be repeated in subsequent semesters increasing in difficulty and use.

Standards of Language Learning

In order to maintain uniformity for all language learners we use the nationally recognized foreign language standards developed by The American Council on the Teaching of Foreign Languages, (ACTFL). Traditionally, language has been taught mostly in vocabulary lists and grammar rules. These new standards place greater emphasis actually using the language. You'll be pleased to know that Power-Glide courses fit these standards exceptionally well. This packet contains a list of what those standards are and how Power-Glide courses effectively meet those standards.

Lesson Plans

Lesson plans are included to help give direction and encouragement as you progress through the course work. The lesson plans provide an approximate time line to keep you focused on the goal of language acquisition. It is important to note that these are guides to help you through the self-paced course; some learners may spend more time and some less. Do whatever is most effective for you.

The lesson plans divide the course work into four semesters. This design will help you gain the appropriate credit for the work you have put forth. Each semester has 3 sections. There are 12 total sections that equal two years worth of work on a public education level. Each section is approximately a month's worth of study and activities if the learner spends 5 days a week studying 20-40 minutes per day. We recognize that some learners will obtain this goal faster and some slower. We encourage you to progress at a rate that is personally comfortable but still challenging.

CD-ROM and Web Site

The lesson plans integrate the CD-ROM and the Power-Glide web site which both include important resources for exploring culture, practicing activities and taking tests. These resources also help provide a multi-sensory learning experience.

Tests and Quizzes

Self-quizzes and self-tests are interspersed throughout the workbook to help learners gain confidence in their language ability. These quizzes and tests are designed to assess areas of strength and weakness. There are three online progress tests and three written tests per semester that correspond to the sections and activities in the lesson plans. These tests will provide progress information for those evaluating your work. As you pursue credit, the progress tests will prepare you to take semester tests.

Note: Answer keys for written tests are located at the end of each section. Remove the answers while taking a test or otherwise insure the integrity of the test by not using the keys during or before testing.

How to Receive Credit

Earning high school credit for foreign language through Power-Glide is very simple. You can receive up to two full years of credit if you complete the entire two year course and the challenge process for each year. If for some reason you only need a semester of credit, you can choose to complete the semester requirements for .5 credit. You will pay a challenge fee when you turn in your portfolio and before receiving your exam. The following steps outline the challenge process:

Challenge Process

- Work through the course using the Academic Guide and course materials. Make sure to take the written tests in the Academic Guide as well as the online progress tests. The progress tests are a tool available to you to check on your progress, and you can take them as many times as you would like. The answers for the written tests are at the end of the Academic Guide.
- Complete the portfolio requirements as outlined below.
- Send your completed portfolio and challenge fee to: Power-Glide Attn: Registrar 1682 West 820 North, Provo, UT 84601. Please include the following information: your name, phone number, social security number (for your transcript), name and address of your proctor, and the year (or semester) for which you are challenging for credit.
- The registrar will send your final test to your proctor. Complete your final test and return it to Power-Glide. A certified teacher will issue a grade based on your portfolio and final test and will return your portfolio with your report card.

Portfolio Requirements

Semester (.5 credit)

- 2-4 minute prepared presentation on video, with the learner speaking something original and creative in the target language. The student can re-tell a story in his/her own words, write an original play, song, poem and then tell or recite it. At the beginning of the audio or video, state name, which course credit is being sought, and the title of the presentation. Example: My name is John Doe. I am seeking credit for Spanish 1. The title of my presentation is a recitation of "The Three Little Pigs."
- 5-6 page research paper in English on a country in which the target language is spoken. The body of the essay should be 3-4 pages with the addition of a title page and bibliography page. The paper should be in a 12-point Times New Roman or equivalent font and double-spaced.
- Two creative projects using the target language and a summary of the experience. For ideas on creative projects, go to www.power-glide.com/school/portfolioideas.asp
- 2-4 page narrative, mini-story plot, or adventure using the target language. This should show a variety of language learning and should be more than just a dialogue between two people. Use 12-point Times New Roman or equivalent font and double space.
- 3 written tests from the Academic Guide. The written tests are a measure of progress in the course and should be graded by the student.

Year (1 credit)
- Two Prepared Presentations: 2-4 minute demonstrations of something original and creative in the target language. The student can re-tell a story in his/her own words, write an original play, song, poem and then tell or recite it. At the beginning of the audio or video, the learner will state his/her name, which course credit is being sought, and the title of the presentation.
- 6-7-page research paper in English on a country in which the target language is spoken. The body of the essay should be 4-5 pages with the addition of a title page and bibliography page. The paper should be in a 12-point Times New Roman or equivalent font and double- spaced.
- Three creative projects using the target language and a summary of the experience. For ideas on creative projects, go to www.power-glide.com/school/portfolioideas.asp
- 2-4 page narrative, mini-story plot, or adventure using the target language. This should show a variety of language learning and should be more than just a dialogue between two people. Use 12-point Times New Roman or equivalent font and double space.
- 6 written tests from the Academic Guide. The written tests are a measure of progress in the course and should be graded by the student.

Scope and Sequence

This French course covers a wide range of vocabulary content and grammar. The material is not organized in units but rather in a sequence of increasing difficulty for both vocabulary content and grammar structures. Below is a list of vocabulary content and grammar taught in the Power-Glide French I and French II Courses.

French 1, Semester 1

Grammar	Vocabulary Content
Identification sentence patterns	Greetings
Noun/Adjective agreement with gender	Introductions
French pronunciation	Family Words
Direct articles and indirect article	Interrogative words
Verbs: intransitive and transitive	Geometric shapes
Nouns	Numbers 1-100, 1000
Read systematically	Adjectives
Prepositions	Animals
Sentence patterns	Sizes
Reading	Story Plots
Comprehension	Body parts
Descriptions	Cause and effects
Possessive pronouns	Culture
Masculine and feminine nouns with articles	Alphabet
Plural article agreement	Instructions
Pronouns and pronouns as objects	Express likes
Translations	Classroom objects
Turn statements into questions	Colors

French 1, Semester 1

Grammar	Vocabulary Content
Listening comprehension	Desires
Speaking Fluency	Sequencing
Reading Comprehension	Create own sentences
Re-tell Stories	Sequencing
Rapid Oral Translations for fluency	Proverbs
Cognate Spelling	Comparisons
Affirmative and negative forms	Recipes

French 1, Semester 2 includes all of the grammar and content in Semester 1 and builds with the following additions.

French 1, Semester 2

Grammar	Vocabulary Content
Context Inference	Stories
Verb tenses	Directions
Error detection	A joke
Verb infinitives and base forms	Geography
Demonstrative pronouns	Instructions
Pronouns	Commands
Locations	Numbers 100-900
Plurals	Descriptions
Action verbs	Mini-story plots
Auxiliary verbs	Conversations
Conjunctions	Problem solving
Imperatives	Culture
Rejoinders	More Shapes
Prepositions	Anticipate answers to questions
Conjugations	Poems
Aspects of tensing	Useful phrases

French 1, Semester 2

Grammar	Vocabulary Content
Concrete objects and associated verbs	Compare and contrast
Places and associated verbs	Word Nuances
Irregular verbs	Proverbs
Composing	
Listening and reading comprehension	
Adjectives and adverbs	
Possessive and reflexive pronouns	

The Power-Glide method is to continue building on a foundation. French 2 builds on the content and grammar principles used in French 1. Here is a list of additional content and grammar that is introduced in French 2.

French 2, Semester 1

Grammar	Vocabulary Content
Pronouns with finite and infinite verbs	Geometry vocabulary
Use of negative voice	Telephone conversations
Pronoun verb use	Small talk
Use object with command voice	Conversations
Past perfect tense	Vocabulary from readings
Verb distinctions	Written and oral creation of stories
Imperfect tense	Ask and answer various types of questions
Recognize common French proverbs	Give and follow instructions
Immediate future tense/ simple future tense	Identify objects from descriptions
New aspects of past tense	Animals
Reading comprehension	Locations
Reflexive pronouns	Size and shape comparison
Natural vs. arbitrary gender	Problem solving
	Geography vocabulary
	Emotion vocabulary
	Culture

French 2, semester 2 is a time for students to master vocabulary and grammar skills through various learning strategies. All of the grammar and vocabulary introduced before this semester is also used and built upon. Here is a list of grammar and content that is in addition to what the student has already learned.

French 2, Semester 2

Grammar	Vocabulary Content
Build grammar skills through readings	Stories and Fables
Past participle	Proverbs
Gain fluency through repetition	Small talk
Irregular past participles	Culture
Indicative verb forms	Mini dialogues
Present perfect	Questions and answers
Preterit past perfect	Useful phrases
Imperfect past perfect	Recipes
Future Perfect	Animals
Conditional	Emotions
Present Subjunctive perfect	Useful everyday words

Power-Glide Methodology

How Power-Glide Differs from Traditional Language Study

Old Practices Produced Unacceptable Results

For most of the last century, language instruction has focused on memorized lists and grammar rules. Although this teaching strategy is objective and easy to grade, the results are rarely satisfactory. After years of study, students fail to communicate even very basic ideas in the foreign language.

Changes Had to be Made

Dr. Robert Blair and other innovative teachers around the world conducted studies involving these learning techniques and recognized that learning a language is not the result of memorizing lists of words and grammar rules.

Standards emphasize changes

In 1993, a coalition of four national language organizations including the American Council on the Teaching of Foreign Languages (ACTFL) assigned an eleven-member task force, representing a variety of languages, levels of instruction, program models, and geographic regions, to define what students should know and be able to do in foreign language education.

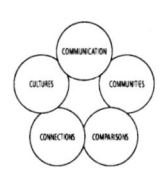

In 1996, this committee came out with The Standards for Foreign Language Learning, five points focused on communication and understanding. Whereas prior to these standards foreign language education was mostly non-creative, the ACTFL standards focus on using language creatively and spontaneously in a variety of ways. These standards can be summarized as follows:

1. Communication - Students should be able to communicate in the language they study.
2. Cultures - Students should gain knowledge and understanding of other cultures.
3. Connections - Students should learn to connect with other disciplines.
4. Comparisons - Students should develop insight into the nature of language and culture.
5. Communities - Students should participate in multilingual communities at home and around the world.

Power-Glide courses have been designed with communication as the primary goal. Our courses embrace these standards and encourage learners to look beyond the old methods of language learning. In order to illustrate how Power-Glide's methodology differs from the old beliefs of foreign language learning, we have designed the following table.

Old Beliefs: Traditional Language Study	Our Beliefs: Power-Glide / ACTFL
Languages are learned mainly through imitation.[1] (1st Myth, p161)	Language is learned through creative, spontaneous speech.
Teachers should present grammatical rules one at a time, and learners should practice examples of each one before going on to another.[1] (7th Myth, p165)	Language learning is not simply linear in development. Grammar is best learned through discovery.
Learners' errors should be corrected as soon as they are made in order to prevent the formation of bad habits.[1] (9th Myth, p167)	Mistakes are okay in the Power-Glide methodology. As a learner develops natural language acquisition and becomes a participant in the language community, mistakes will naturally disappear. When it is appropriate, correctness is emphasized.
Teachers should use materials that expose students only to language structures which they have already been taught.[1] (10th Myth, p168)	Learners should be exposed to multiple language structures at different levels.

[1] Lightbrown, P.M. and Spada, N. (1999). How Language Are Learned. Oxford: Oxford University Press.

Power-Glide and the ACTFL standards are designed to help students use language creatively and spontaneously. Instead of telling you the rules, Power-Glide activities enable you to discover them for yourself. This is what makes Power-Glide truly unique.

One student wrote:
I took five quarters of French in college. If I could see it, I could make some sense of it. But still, I could not carry on a conversation. I didn't have a feel for the language, nor any confidence to express myself vocally. After three class sessions with Power-Glide, I found myself last week suddenly speaking out whole spontaneous thoughts in class. They were not pattern sentences from a book. They were my own. They weren't all correct. But they were comprehensible. I felt like I had broken through a barrier! I was beginning to think in French and somehow had confidence to speak without being sure it was all perfect.

If you use the course the way it's designed, this will be your experience, too. You will enjoy language learning, meet the national standards and be strides ahead of traditional learners.

Our courses are composed of an adventure story platform, a wide variety of activities- each one challenging in a different way, a variety of sensory approaches, and a philosophy that says:

- The goal is meaningful conversation springing from creative thought in the target language.
- It is okay to make mistakes. We get better by practice, not by being afraid to try.
- It is okay to use something before it is perfect.
- It is okay to move on before fully understanding. Much of the information will come your way again.
- It is not okay to fail to try. Language is a contact sport, not a mental exercise.
- Discovery is a joyful process. We know that if students are told every step to take, and are given every answer, we invite shallow learning and rob them of something essential. Instead, we invite them to think and discover language for themselves.

Sample Test

Knowing the types of questions that my appear on a test is helpful. This section provides a few examples of the testing method used in the Power-Glide Foreign Language School semester tests.

Listening Section

Pictograph/Frame Identification Example

Instructions: For each question you will hear a descriptive statement. Choose the answer from the frame that best fits the description.

(Audio: "Quel cadre contient une étoile, un cercle et un carré?")

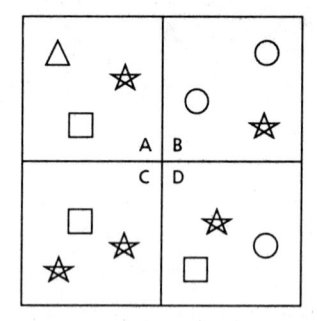

Conversation Completions Example

Instructions: Listen to the following conversation and choose the best answer that completes the conversation.

(Audio: "'Qui est cette fille?'
    'C'est ma soeur.'
    'Comment s'appelle-t-elle?'
    'Son nom est Rose.'
    'D'où vient-elle?'")

a. 'Niece'
b. 'Quebec'
c. 'Happy'
d. 'Today'

Comprehension Example

Instructions: Listen to the passage and answer the questions that follows.

(Audio: "Que fait la reine? Elle joue du piano. Et la princesse? Elle chante avec le prince dans la tour. Et le roi? Il joue du tambour avec le chat et le chien. Ils sont tous contents!")

1. Que fait le prince?
    a. Elle joue du piano
    b. Elles chantent
    c. Il chante
    d. Ils jouent

2. Qui est dans la tour?
    a. La reine
    b. Le prince et la princesse

c. Le roi
   d. Le chien et le chat

Instructions: Listen to the following mini-lecture and answer the questions.

(Audio: "Qu'est-ce qu'un alphabet? Un alphabet est composé de lettres. Il y a plusieurs alphabets: l'alphabet grec, arabe, russe, romain, etc. Les lettres d'un alphabet représentent les sons d'une langue. Par exemple, les lettres de l'alphabet français représentent les sons du français. L'alphabet du français et de l'anglais contient vingt-six lettres. Il y a cinq voyelles et vingt-et-une consonnes.")

1. Quel son représente les lettres de l'alphabet anglais?
   a. Russe
   b. Anglais
   c. Grec
   d. Français

2. Combien de voyelles contient l'alphabet français?
   a. 12
   b. 21
   c. 5
   d. 26

Reading/Vocabulary Section

Picture Identification Example

Instructions: Choose the statement that is represented by the pictograph.

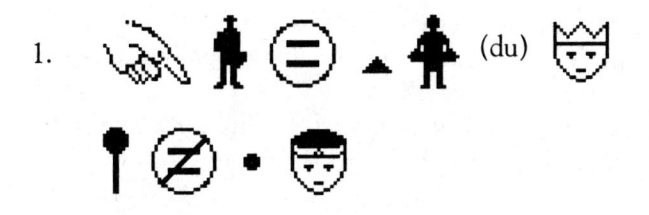

1.
   a. Cet homme est un roi. Il n'est pas un prince.
   b. Ce prince est le serviteur du roi. Il est un homme.
   c. Cet homme est le serviteur du roi. Il n'est pas un prince.
   d. Ce roi est un homme. Il n'est pas un serviteur.

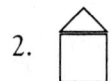

2.
   a. Ce sont trois lignes verticales.
   b. Un triangle au-dessus d'un carré.
   c. Le carré est plus petit que le triangle.
   d. Ces figures sont de la même forme.

Instructions: Write T or F for each statement describing the pictograph.

____ 1. Toutes ces lignes sont parallèles.
____ 2. Ces figures sont quatre triangles.
____ 3. Ces lignes sont courbes.
____ 4. Ces lignes perpendiculaires sont des lettres.

Diglot-weave Example

Instructions: Fill in the blanks with either nouns, verbs, or adjectives. If they are nouns, the article in French will be provided.

Example: Fill in the blanks with the French word that best completes the sentence.

I would like vous raconter une 1._____. It is about d' un roi and d' une 2._____ and leur enfant, le petit 3._____. L' enfant likes to play à la 4._____ avec son chien. They 5._____ dans la cour du royaume. Le petit prince kicks la balle very hard and high in the air. The ball lands on the roof du 6._____ next de la 7._____ of the living room. Ouff!! The little prince soupire très fort! Il n a pas 8._____ the window. Le chien moves his tail to show au petit prince that he is content. The dog and the little prince 9._____ de bons amis. The king and the queen sont 10._____ de leur petit garcon.

Reading Comprehenion Example

Instructions: Read the passage and then choose the best answer for each question.

Le Canada se trouve au nord des Etats-Unis. L'Europe se trouve de l'autre côté de l'Atlantique.
L'Europe se divise en deux: il y a l'est et l'ouest. En Europe de l'ouest se trouvent un grand nombre de pays: la Grèce, l'Italie, la Suisse, la Finlande, la Suède, la Norvège, le Danemark,
l'Allemagne, l'Espagne, la France, les Pays-Bas et l'Angleterre. Que de nombreux pays! En Europe de l'est se trouvent aussi plusieurs pays: la Roumanie, la Yougoslavie, la Bulgarie, la Hongrie, la Tchécoslovaquie et la Pologne. Sans oublier une partie de la Russie.

1. Quel pays se trouve en Europe de l'est?
    a. L'Espagne
    b. La Suède
    c. La Russie
    d. Le Danemark

2. Quel pays se trouve au nord des Etats-Unis?
    a. L'Angleterre
    b. Le Canada
    c. La France
    d. L'Italie

3. Où est situé le Canada?
    a. Nord

b. Ouest
   c. Sud
   d. Est

4. Combien de pays se trouvent en Europe de l'ouest?
   a. 6
   b. 12
   c. 9
   d. 7

5. Dans quelle Europe fait partie la Russie?
   a. Europe du nord
   b. Europe de l'est
   c. Europe de l'ouest
   d. Europe du sud

Structure Section

Grammaticality Judgement Example

Instructions: Read the sentences and decide if it is grammatically correct or not correct (you do not need to make corrections).

C - Correct
I - Incorrect

____ 1. C'est l'histoire au sujet d'un royaume.
____ 2. La reine aiment jouer du piano.
____ 3. Le roi joues du tambour tous les jours.
____ 4. Le prince chante la princesse dans la salle de bains.
____ 5. Le chat aime joué du tambour dans la tour.
____ 6. Le chien n'aime la musique.
____ 7. Le roi n'est pas content.
____ 8. Le roi vont mettre le chien dans la tour.
____ 9. Le chat et le chien joue du tambour ensemble.
____ 10. La reine va chanter et jouet du piano dans une pièce du royaume.

Translation Examples

Instructions: Translate the following from English to French.

1. The famous king has the key of the kingdom.

   _____

Instructions: Translate the following from French to English.

2. La princesse va pleurer seule dans la salle de bains.

   _____

Scatterchart Example

Instructions: Using the words in the scatterchart create five sentences. Use a word as many times as you need.

---

petite(s)   longue(s)
                        voici   la/les
cette/ces   c'est
        chose(s)   est/sont
                        une/des
autre(s)   noire(s)
                            blanche(s)

---

1. _____

2. _____

3. _____

4. _____

5. _____

Lesson Plans

If you are seeking credit for this course, review the "Pursuing Credit" information in the Overview at the beginning of this Guide. You will need to have a completed portfolio according to the specifications in the Overview.

Keep these tips in mind as you work through each section:

1. After you finish a lesson, mark the square (□) to the left of the lesson number. This will help you remember where to start next time.
2. Symbols indicating the materials you will need for each lesson are listed to the right of the lesson number.

    ▯ = Your workbook

    🔊 = Audio (cassettes or audio CD's)

    ⊙ = CD-ROM

    †† = Internet activity or research

    ⚲ = Internet progress test

    ✓ = Written test
3. Read the instructions carefully for every activity.
4. Repeat aloud all the French words you hear on the audio or CD-ROM. This will help you become accustomed to the production of the new sounds.
5. Go at your own pace, the lesson plan is a guide to help you pace yourself.
6. Have fun with your activities and practice your new language skills with others.
7. Record yourself speaking French on a tape so you can evaluate your own speaking progress.
8. Record your progress in your journal so you can identify your growth in the target language.
9. Prepare an academic portfolio file where you can save work that you will do throughout the course.
10. Written tests and answer keys are found following the lesson plans for their respective semesters. To maintain the integrity of the tests, do not use the answer keys while testing.

French 1, Semester 1

Isn't learning another language exciting? I'm excited that you are learning French. Have fun with this course and enjoy the process of learning.

Section 1

You are about to embark on the most exciting adventure of your life. This section is approximately one month's worth of activities and study.

After completing this section you will be able to:

- Use words and phrases for introductions and greetings.
- Identify word breaks in French.
- Use articles, plurals, and noun/adjective agreement with gender.
- Pronounce French vowels, semi-vowels, nasal sound, and consonant sounds correctly.
- Comprehend, understand, and perform instructions using numbers, points, lines and figures.
- Use and say numbers 1-10, 100's and 1000's.
- Develop speed and fluency in spontaneous speech using interrogatives.
- String together your own narratives.
- Read a diglot weave story.
- Gain information and appreciation for other cultures.

Let's begin.

☐ Lesson 1-1

Turn to activity #1, in your workbook. Follow instructions and pay close attention to everything you will need to know in order to complete your assignment on l'ile de Providence. Pause the audio as needed so you don't miss anything new. At the end of activity #1, do the self-test. How many

Journal/Notes:

ings and introduction words can you say? You'll have additional opportunities throughout the course to review and use these phrases. What do you think you will have to learn in order to find the treasure?

☐ 1-2 ☐

Do you like solving mysteries? Turn to Activity #2 and work on various puzzles that will help you crack the code of French. As you discover how French works, you will begin to formulate your own sentences and not just repeat memorized phrases. This activity has 4 parts and a challenge. Carefully work through each part discovering unique aspects of the language. When each part is no longer a mystery to you, move to the next one. The challenge section focuses on pronunciation. Work through this challenge until you feel comfortable enough to move forward. Recognize that the entire course will help you with your pronunciation and that this challenge is designed to set you in the right direction.

☐ 1-3 ☐ 🔊

Turn to activity #3. This activity is a continuation of activity #2. Listen to the puzzle sentences. Make connections to English. How is listening to the French without the English to read making a difference in your understanding? If you need to write your English approximations down, go ahead. Do whatever you need to make connections with your new language.

☐ 1-4 ☐ ⊙

Turn to activity #4 in your workbook. This is a short self-test focusing on translations from French to English and English to French. You should have time explore the CD-ROM and create one of your own adventures with "La Mouche."

☐ 1-5 ☐

It's time to add numbers to your vocabulary. You may already know numbers 1-10 in French but activity #7 will help you listen for these numbers to solve problems. This activity contains exercises A-F. Exercise D is a little tricky so this additional information may help. The frames are all lettered A-J. Inside each frame there are four sections labeled A, B, C, and D. For each frame there are at least 3 identification problems. You will hear the answer after a short pause. The answer is a letter corresponding to the section of a frame. Do not go on to the next frame until you have heard at least three questions. The pace of the audio is rather fast, so use your pause button if you need to. Repeat the exercise until you feel comfortable with your responses. How can learning this information help you in your adventures with "La Mouche"?

☐ 1-6 ☐

Creative Portfolio Project: Make the Quiche Lorraine recipe in your workbook (end of activity #5). If you have friends who also speak French, or you study with other learners, make this together. Speak French as you shop for the ingredients and

Journal/Notes:

prepare the meal. Use whatever language skills you have and enjoy a fun time. Look for ways to use your language. This is just a sample of what you can do. You may have a more creative idea. Whatever you do, write about it and put the summary in your academic portfolio file.

☐ 1-7

Did you enjoy your creative culture project? Let's do some more with numbers. Turn to activity #6 in your workbook. Follow the instructions given for this exercise. The pneumonic helps in this activity will key your memory to use correct pronunciation with the proper French word. How many seconds will it take you to say all the numbers?

☐ 1-8

Turn to activity #7 in your workbook and follow instructions for each section of the activity. You may want to use one study session for each section of this activity. You should be able to do some rapid translations from English to French and French to English when you are finished. You have some timed exercises in this section so get your watch ready. You are also exposed to some new vocabulary. Remember not to get hung up if you can't remember new words. Keep studying and your language will progress like a native.

☐ 1-9

How did your oral translations go? Remember, don't get frustrated, keep moving. You are equipped with an amazing ability to learn another language! Turn to activity #8 and learn how to begin formulating sentences in French. Complete this activity through task 3.

☐ 1-10

At the end of activity #8 the adventure continues and you will begin your cultural exploration. Read the facts and figures on the French speaking world and the cultural overviews of Algeria and Belgium. For additional research on these two countries explore http://www.power-glide.com/french/links. Keep notes and bibliography information in case you want to do your portfolio research paper on either of these two countries. Try to think of what is most interesting to you. A good research paper will include information that is intriguing to the writer. You will need to spend more than one study session researching and writing your paper, but you can do that throughout the entire semester and it doesn't have to be done before you move to the next activity.

☐ 1-11

Your adventure is about to take another turn. Open your workbook to activity #9. Learn how to map your thoughts in French. You will use some nonsense sentences as you go through these activities but that only heightens your ability to map your thoughts in French. Have fun with it and use it as a springboard to creating your own innovative conversations.

Journal/Notes:

☐ **1-12**

Today you are going to become familiar with the term "diglot-weave" and how to use it. Turn to activity #10 in your workbook. Read the information about a diglot-weave but don't begin reading the story. Before reading the story go to the CD-ROM and click on the interactive window. Do the primer and the match and learn activity for "The Broken Window." This activity may take a few minutes or an entire study session depending on your abilities. When you feel comfortable with your new vocabulary go to 1-13.

☐ **1-13**

Turn to activity #10 and #11 in your workbook and read and listen to the diglot-weave with the audio. You should recognize the vocabulary you learned on the CD-ROM and even pick up a few new words. How many of the words introduced can you remember and use in other forms of speech? Tell someone a few of the new words and phrases you learned from this story.

☐ **1-14**

Listen to the story of "The Broken Window" again. This time go to the CD-ROM and listen to the narrative with the picture prompts. The interactive narrative is divided into shorter reading segments. Review each page as needed with and without picture prompts. The goal is to see if you understand more vocabulary the second or third time through.

☐ **1-15**

You are now ready for your first progress test. You will take this test online. Before you take the test your may want to review the self-quizzes and tests, toward fluency activities and anything else you may not be confident in. Can you meet the objectives of the section? If you can, make a note of that in your journal and know that you are ready to take the progress test.

☐ **1-16**

Take online progress test #1. Go to http://www.power-glide.com/progresstests. You will need to enter your name and e-mail address. When you receive your progress test results review the items you missed and then get ready for the written test.

☐ **1-17**

Take written test #1. Have it corrected and put the results in your academic portfolio file.

☐ **1-18**

It's always nice to relax after a test and have fun. Go to the CD-ROM, click on La Mouche and have fun with an adventure. Pay attention to the French and concentrate on how much you can understand. Have fun and enjoy the activity.

Journal/Notes:

Section 2

Can you believe that you know so much French already? Are you ready to continue your learning adventure?

After completing this section you will be able to:

- Use numbers 11-16 alone and in combination with thousands.
- Increase usage of adjectives with nouns.
- Recognize sentence patterns and build comprehension skills.
- Increase fluency.
- Think and communicate in French using targeted vocabulary.
- Recognize words that are familiar to you as you read.
- Say nouns and adjectives in various types of sentences.
- Use pictographs to reinforce vocabulary and listening skills.
- Enhance skill of masculine and feminine nouns with various forms of articles.
- Use singular and plural article agreement with regular and irregular verbs.
- Increase pronunciation skills
- Expand cultural awareness and knowledge.
- Comprehend and understand the main idea when listening to a story or conversation.
- String together your own narratives and create stories.
- Conjugate verbs in present and past tense.
- Develop speed and fluency in using interrogatives.

☐ **Lesson 2-1**

Are you ready for more numbers? Turn to activity #12 and practice saying very large numbers in French. Maybe the treasure you find in your adventure will have some big numbers that you will need to identify. Practice until you can say the string of numbers very rapidly.

☐ **2-2**

Turn to activity #13 in your workbook. Here are some more points, lines, and figures. With this activity you will learn some new adjectives. Read the instructions and do each piece of the activity. Remember the answer in the multiple-choice frames comes after the question, it isn't part of the next question. When you feel comfortable with your comprehension move to the next activity.

☐ **2-3**

It is one skill to speak French and it is another to really think in French. Turn to activity #14, part 1 in your workbook and train your brain to think in French. You've already had some exposure to this type of lesson. Avoid thinking about this activity in English. Stick to thinking in French. This will take some practice but you can do it.

Journal/Notes:

☐ 2-4

Turn to activity #14, part 2 and continue using pictures and sentence building blocks to think in French.

☐ 2-5

Now that you've learned a little about thinking in French, let's use that skill in the next activity. Turn to activity #15 and follow the specific instructions for each section. Whenever you're asked to translate from English to French, remember to do the translation orally. Stay away from writing the translation down before speaking. Write the translations after you have done the oral exercise.

☐ 2-6

With all the practice you've had in the last few days with training your brain to think in French, this next activity will be a snap. Turn to activity #16 in your workbook. Here are some more pictographs. Try to focus on the French meaning without thinking of the English first. Remember that the actual words aren't as important as the part of speech they represent in the sentence structure.

☐ 2-7

Were you able to say all your pictograph sentences in French? Do you understand how each word fits into French sentence structure? Turn to activity #17 and focus more on grammar. There are 8 parts to this activity so it may take you several study sessions to complete these parts. Remember to translate orally before you ever try to write down the translations. Producing the translations orally will help you have greater fluency in your speech. Writing the translations will help your reading skills.

☐ 2-8

Activity #18 works some of the unique pronunciations of French. Listen to the audio and practice these sounds until you sound like a native. Read the adventure and move on.

☐ 2-9

It's time for some more culture. Turn to page 60 in your workbook and read a quick overview on Quebec. Search the web site and/or CD-ROM for more information. If you desire to write your research paper on Quebec, take notes and make sure you have bibliography information filed in your academic portfolio file. If you are seeking credit, remember to keep working on your research paper all semester!

☐ 2-10

Activity #19 is a short story that will help you with your French comprehension and production. Listen to the story in French first and identify the picture prompts to their French equivalents. Turn to the second page and follow instructions in the learning activity section.

Journal/Notes:

☐ 2-11

Activity #20 is a change of pace, using points, lines, and figures again. Review the scatter chart and then do each section of the activity. Pause the audio as needed. You should be familiar with this activity, so have fun. Remember to read more on your adventure. Are you keeping all your clues in one place so you can solve the mystery?

☐ 2-12

How are you doing on your comprehension? Let's stretch your ability a little farther. Turn to activity #21 in your workbook. Work on making grammar connections in French and don't rely so much on your English rules. Don't forget to do the tasks at the end of the activity.

☐ 2-13

Did you have fun creating your own sentences? Turn to activity #22 in your workbook and prepare yourself to create more sentences. Remember that the overall goal of this activity is to help you think in French. There are a lot of pictures, so you might need more than one study session to remember the vocabulary.

☐ 2-14

Turn to activity #23 in your workbook. You'll notice that the entire activity is done without audio. Go through each language focus until you feel confident with the information. This may take you several study sessions. Don't let the study of this material become tedious. If it does, take a break and come back to it another time.

☐ 2-15

Turn to activity #24 and work on a self-test. Follow the instructions and work toward proficiency in each section. Remember it's okay to make mistakes. Making mistakes means that you are willing to use your language and will progress forward. You will also learn to recognize your own errors and discover how to correct them as you continue to learn. Do your best and then move to the next activity.

☐ 2-16

What would you say in French in order to find out information? Turn to activity #25 and work on interrogatives. Use the pictures to help you remember the words in French. Focus on the French translations and how they are used more than you focus on English.

☐ 2-17

Do you think it is possible for you to use what you know in French and create a story at this point? Turn to activity #26 and learn how to generate your own sentences and connect them together to make a story.

Journal/Notes:

☐ 2-18

Using the information you learned in activity #26, turn to activity #27 and create your own story. Make your story as creative as you can. You may want to use this activity as one of your assignments for your portfolio.

☐ 2-19

It's time to prepare for progress test #2. You have learned all you need to know to do well on this test. Prepare for your test by going over your self-tests. Focus on question forms, verb forms, and the conversations you've been learning. Go over things that you had a difficult time with and make them solid in your mind before taking the test.

☐ 2-20

Take progress test #2. Go to http://www.power-glide.com/progresstests. Read each question carefully and try to understand the meaning before answering. Don't get discouraged if you don't know the answer right off; try going on to another question and them come back to the one that was confusing—the answer will come to you.

☐ 2-21

Review the items you may have missed on your progress test. When you feel comfortable with what you've learned, take written test #2. Have it corrected and put the results in your academic portfolio file.

Section 3

When you complete this section you will be halfway through French 1. Wow! Stop and think how much you are learning and how much fun it is.

After completing this section you will be able to:

- Identify and say directional symbols, upward, downward, right, left, below, between, and pointing.
- Read and comprehend meaning of a text.
- Use vocabulary from readings to increase your speaking fluency.
- Add body parts to your vocabulary base.
- Expand cultural awareness.
- String together narratives.
- Recognize sentence patterns and structures.
- Re-tell stories using visuals.
- Use geography vocabulary.
- Count using decade and teen numbers in combination with 100's and 1000's.
- Use sentence building blocks to think in French.
- Understand more about the French alphabet.
- Understand grammar rules and how they relate to your language skills.
- Communicate with limited vocabulary.
- Ask questions and understand answers.
- Use correct verb tenses.

Journal/Notes:

- -

- -

- -

- -

- -

☐ Lesson 3-1

Turn to activity #28 in your workbook where you will find some more points, lines, and figures. You know how this lesson works, so jump right in. Notice that as you understand and perform the instructions given in this lesson, your brain is making significant strides at thinking in French.

☐ 3-2

It's time to learn some vocabulary for body parts. Pull up the CD-ROM and click on the interactive button. When you get to the interactive screen, click on the Body-Parts primer. When you feel comfortable with all the names of the body parts in French, move on to the Match and Learn exercise. You've done an activity like this before, so you can practice identifying the body parts by clicking them with the mouse. Do this activity until you can identify each part correctly and then move on.

☐ 3-3

Now that you know body part vocabulary, turn to activity #29 in your workbook. This activity is a simple conversation that will help you understand new vocabulary in an easy context. Listen to the audio as many times as necessary. Try this activity with a young child and see how many French words you can teach them. Write about your teaching experience for one of your creative projects.

☐ 3-4

On page 91 of your workbook there are some culture questions for you to answer and some quick facts on France. For more research information, look on the CD-ROM and http://www.power-glide.com/french/links. If you choose to do a research paper on France, take notes and record your bibliography information. Remember, you don't have to do the research and writing of the paper all at once. Keep your information in case you want to do a research paper on France.

Creative Activity: On page 92, there is a recipe for baguettes, or French Bread. Make the bread with family and friends and discuss why the French eat this type of bread.

☐ 3-5

Turn to activity #30 and focus on new vocabulary you can use to create sentences. Remember that you are training your brain to think in French. Use the English to see if you understand French, but don't get caught up in trying to translate literally.

☐ 3-6

Turn to activity #31 in your workbook. This activity is a simulation of a French classroom. As you listen to the audio try to imagine yourself in this situation for real. What would you do to gain greater understanding of what the teacher was saying? Because you have an audio recording and a printed text you can go back and listen again and read the printed text. How would you learn this

Journal/Notes:

information if you didn't have that advantage? You would probably attach French names to the physical objects that were used as visual cues. Then you would repeat the French word either aloud or in your mind each time you saw the physical object. Gather the objects described in this lesson and listen to the audio again. Touch the object as it is being said. After you've listened to the audio with the physical objects, try to teach something about those objects you just learned.

☐ 3-7

Turn to activity #32. This activity is similar to #31 but the information is more complex. You may want to use a map to make necessary connections. Some words are cognates so you shouldn't have much trouble with them. Focus on comprehending in French. Using the French you learn from this activity, tell another person at least two geography facts. Continue reading the adventure and collecting clues.

☐ 3-8

Turn to activity #33 and work on decade numbers with 100's and 1000's. Use the phonetic approximations to help you key your memory of the French word and pronunciation. Make a goal to say all your number strings within 15 seconds.

☐ 3-9

Today you will learn some new pictographs to help build your French sentence patterns. Turn to activity #34. Go through each part thoroughly.

Journal/Notes:

Focus on French and work toward saying each sentence without hesitation. At the end of this activity create some of your own sentences using the pictographs provided. You can also make your own flashcards of the pictographs to help you create sentences or play games.

☐ 3-10

Have you ever wondered where the alphabet comes from? Turn to activity #35 and listen to a lecture on the history of the French alphabet. Don't focus on translating the lecture. Focus on gaining the main idea and being able to express that to another person.

☐ 3-11

Turn to activity #36. This activity is similar to other conversations found in "Chatter at a Royal Ball." However, this time you must focus on listening and not reading from pictographs. Prepare for the conversation by going through the vocabulary words and then apply your knowledge while listening to the conversation in French. Don't worry if you don't understand all of the dialogue without the pictures. It may take some time but keep moving forward.

☐ 3-12

Take some time to focus on distinctive parts of grammar so you can increase your language proficiency. Turn to activity #37 and work through each grammar focus until you feel comfortable with it and can say the sentences in the oral translations without hesitation.

☐ **3-13**

Activity #38 is another diglot-weave story. It is part one of a story. As you listen to the story, make connections and links in English that will help you retain the new French vocabulary. Listen to the story as many times as you like, each time focusing on new vocabulary and how you are going to use these new words in your speech.

☐ **3-14**

Activity #39 is the second part of the story, "The Key of the King's Kingdom." Notice how the story has become more complex. Use the pictures to help you tell the story again with more complexity. Can you add anything additional to your version of the story? Use what you've learned and see how much you can embellish the story.

☐ **3-15**

Have you ever wondered how to communicate when you can't say everything you want to? Turn to activity #40 and practice using the phrases and sentence examples to communicate with limited means. Try creating as many of your own sentences as you can.

☐ **3-16**

Activity #41 is another look at grammar patterns. Go through each focus and practice the examples and then create your own until you feel comfortable with the rules. After you translate orally, write the translations from and into French. This activity may take you several days depending on your time and understanding. Take the time you need, remembering that if it becomes tedious, stop and come back to it later.

☐ **3-17**

At the end of activity #41 is a very short culture quiz and a recipe for split pea soup. Take this study opportunity to gather additional culture information on the CD-ROM or web site. You might want to do a creative activity and write about it for your portfolio. Continue with the adventure and collect clues that will help you uncover the mystery. You may also want to continue your adventures with "La Mouche."

☐ **3-18**

I hope you take the opportunity to be creative in your study. Activity #42 is another opportunity to string together your own narratives. Learn the words in the scatter chart and use them to create your own sentences or story. Use your imagination. The more creative you can be with the words you are given, the more likely it is that you will remember them and have spontaneous speech. Remember that you aren't after perfection, you're after communication.

Journal/Notes:

☐ **3-19**

You are now ready for progress test #3. As you have done in the past, review all self-tests, vocabulary, and grammar sections. Can you meet the objectives of this section? Take plenty of time for your review and make sure you are confident with your knowledge before taking the test.

☐ **3-20**

You are now ready to take progress test #3. Go to http://www.power-glide.com/progresstests. Enter your e-mail address and proceed as before. Remember to read each question carefully. When you receive your results, review the items you need to and take the written test for this section.

☐ **3-21**

Take written test #3. Have it corrected and put in your academic portfolio file.

> *If you are seeking credit for this course, review the How to Receive Credit information in the Overview at the beginning of this Guide. You will need to have a completed portfolio according to the specifications in the Overview.*

Journal/Notes:

French Test 1

Name _____
Total _____ /100 points

PART 1
(7 points) Write the English equivalent to the French body parts.

1. *les pieds* _____
2. *les mains* _____
3. *la tête* _____
4. *le visage* _____
5. *le nez* _____
6. *un oeil* _____
7. *la bouche* _____

PART 2
(12 points) Read the sentence and draw what is described.

8.	*Un point.*	
9.	*Une ligne.*	
10.	*Un chiffre, le chiffre un.*	
11.	*Deux points et une ligne.*	
12.	*Trois lignes, deux points, et un chiffre, le chiffre trois.*	
13.	*Trois chiffres, les chiffres trois, deux, et un, et deux lignes.*	
14.	*Quatre points, deux lignes, et un chiffre, le chiffre deux.*	
15.	*Trois lignes et deux chiffres, les chiffres trois et quatre.*	
16.	*Cinq chiffres, les chiffres un, deux, trois, quatre, cinq, et cinq points.*	
17.	*Cinq points et deux lignes.*	
18.	*Une ligne et six points.*	

| 19. | *Six chiffres, les chiffres un, deux, trois, quatre, cinq, et six.* | |

PART 3
(11 points) Match the English sentence with the French translation.

20. _____ Is Nanette a good friend? a. *Ami ou adversaire, qui sait?*

21. _____ I don't know if Nanette is a good friend. b. *C'est bien?*

22. _____ I know who Jacques is. c. *Est-ce que Nanette est une bonne amie?*

23. _____ Me too, I know who Jacques is. d. *Je ne sais pas si Nanette est une bonne amie.*

24. _____ I know well that he is a good friend. e. *Je ne sais pas.*

25. _____ No, Jacques is not a friend, he is a foe. f. *Je sais bien que c'est un bon ami.*

26. _____ Friend or foe, who knows? g. *Je sais qui est Jacques.*

27. _____ I don't know. h. *Moi aussi, je sais qui est Jacques.*

28. _____ Who knows if Jacques is a friend? i. *Non, Jacques n'est pas un ami, c'est un adversaire.*

29. _____ Is that all right? j. *Oui, c'est bien.*

30. _____ Yes, it's fine. k. *Qui sait si Jacques est un ami?*

PART 4
(15 points—3 points for each sentence) Rewrite the sentences below, putting spaces between each of the words.

31. *Unhommeetunefille.*

_____

32. *Marieestunefille.*

_____

33. *Elleestunepetitefille.*

_____

34. *LamèreetlepèredePauletMarie.*

_____

35. *Ilaimeaidersasoeur.*

PART 5

(15 points) Match the English phrase with the French equivalent.

36. _____	It's me.	a.	*Adieu.*
37. _____	Right?	b.	*Après vous, madame.*
38. _____	After you, ma'am.	c.	*Bon voyage!*
39. _____	Thanks much.	d.	*Bonjour.*
40. _____	Have a good trip!	e.	*C'est moi.*
41. _____	Pardon me.	f.	*Comment dit-on...?*
42. _____	You speak well.	g.	*En anglais.*
43. _____	How does one say...?	h.	*En français.*
44. _____	In English.	i.	*Je ne sais pas.*
45. _____	In French.	j.	*Merci beaucoup.*
46. _____	What is this?	k.	*N'est-ce pas?*
47. _____	What does ___ mean?	l.	*Pardonnez-moi.*
48. _____	Hello (good day!).	m.	*Qu'est-ce que c'est?*
49. _____	Goodbye.	n.	*Qu'est-ce que veut dire ___?*
50. _____	I don't know.	o.	*Vous parlez bien.*

PART 6

(10 points) Identify which French translation is correct.

51. _____ They help.
    a. *Ils aident.*
    b. *Ils aide.*

52. _____ She has a brother. Yes, Paul is her brother.
    a. *Elle a un frère. Oui, Paul est sa frère.*
    b. *Elle a un frère. Oui, Paul est son frère.*

53. _____ He has a sister. Yes, Marie is his sister.
    a. *Il a une soeur. Oui, Marie est son soeur.*
    b. *Il a une soeur. Oui, Marie est sa soeur.*

54. _____ Paul likes his sister. Yes, he likes her.
    a. *Paul aime son soeur. Oui, il l'aime.*
    b. *Paul aime sa soeur. Oui, il l'aime.*

55. _____ She likes her brother.
    a. *Elle aime son frère.*
    b. *Elle aime sa frère.*

56. _____ Yes, she likes him.
    a. *Oui, il l'aime.*
    b. *Oui, elle l'aime.*

57. _____ Marie helps her brother. And he helps her.
    a. *Marie aide son frère. Et il l'aide.*
    b. *Marie aide son frère. Et il aide.*

58. _____ They paint together.
    a. *Ils peignent ensemble.*
    b. *Ils peint ensemble.*

59. _____ They cook together.
    a. *Ils cuisinent ensemble.*
    b. *Ils cuisine ensemble.*

60. _____ He likes his sisters. She likes her brothers. a. *Il aime son soeurs. Elle aime sa frères.*
 b. *Il aime ses soeurs. Elle aime ses frères.*

PART 7

(10 points) Read the following sentences and do the math to find the answer. Then write out the number in French in the space below.

Example: *un + un = deux*   (translation: one + one = two)

61. *deux + deux =* _____   66. *deux + trois + cinq =* _____

62. *deux + trois =* _____   67. *six - quatre =* _____

63. *trois + trois =* _____   68. *cinq x deux =* _____

64. *deux + quatre =* _____   69. *dix x cent =* _____

65. *six + quatre =* _____   70. *cinq x dix x deux =* _____

PART 8

(20 points) Choose the French translation that is correct both in grammar and meaning.

71. _____ The things.
 a. *Les choses.*
 b. *La choses.*

72. _____ Some things.
 a. *De choses.*
 b. *Des choses.*

73. _____ Here is a thing.
 a. *Voici une chose.*
 b. *Voici est une chose.*

74. _____ Here is a white thing.
 a. *Voici une chose blanche.*
 b. *Voici une blanche chose.*

75. _____ And here is a black thing.
 a. *Voici une noire chose.*
 b. *Et voici une chose noire.*

76. _____ Here are the things.
 a. *Voici la choses.*
 b. *Voici les choses.*

77. _____ Here are the other things.
 a. *Voici les autres choses.*
 b. *Voici l'autre choses.*

78. _____ Some white things and some black things.
 a. *Des choses blanche et des choses noire.*
 b. *Des choses blanches et des choses noires.*

36

79. _____ One thing is black.
     a. *Une chose est noire.*
     b. *Une chose est noires.*

80. _____ One thing is white, the other is black.
     a. *Une chose sont blanche, l'autre sont noire.*
     b. *Une chose est blanche, l'autre est noire.*

81. _____ The black thing is large.
     a. *La noire chose est grande.*
     b. *La chose noire est grande.*

82. _____ The white thing is small.
     a. *La blanche chose est petite.*
     b. *La chose blanche est petite.*

83. _____ This thing is small and this thing is large.
     a. *Cette chose est petite et cette chose est grande.*
     b. *Ces chose est petite et ces chose est grande.*

84. _____ These things are small.
     a. *Ces choses est petites.*
     b. *Ces choses sont petites.*

85. _____ These small things are white.
     a. *Ces petites choses sont blanches.*
     b. *Ces choses petites est blanches.*

86. _____ These large things are black.
     a. *Ces grandes choses sont noires.*
     b. *Ces choses grandes est noires.*

87. _____ Is the black thing large? Yes.
     a. *Est-ce que la chose noire est grande? Oui.*
     b. *Est la chose noire grande? Oui.*

88. _____ Is the white thing large? No.
     a. *Est la chose blanche grande? Non.*
     b. *Est-ce que la chose blanche est grande? Non.*

89. _____ Are these things large and white? No.
     a. *Ces choses sont grandes et blanches? Non.*
     b. *Est-ce que ces choses sont grandes et blanches? Non.*

90. _____ Are these things small? Yes.
     a. *Est-ce que ces choses sont petites? Oui.*
     b. *Ces choses sont petites? Oui.*

French Test 2

Name _____
Total _____/100 points

Part 1
(10 points) Match the French and English words.

1. _____ un monsieur   a. with
2. _____ une demoiselle   b. a man
3. _____ peut-être   c. here
4. _____ avec   d. where
5. _____ qui   e. a gentleman
6. _____ là   f. the king
7. _____ où   g. who
8. _____ le roi   h. a (young) lady
9. _____ ici   i. there
10. _____ un homme   j. perhaps

Part 2
(10 points) Match the French and English words.

11. _____ la tour   a. a lot
12. _____ le bain   b. the prince
13. _____ la princesse   c. the bath
14. _____ aussi   d. cat
15. _____ le prince   e. in
16. _____ la salle de bains f. the tower
17. _____ mais   g. the princess
18. _____ chat   h. also
19. _____ dans   i. the bathroom
20. _____ beaucoup   j. but

Part 3
(16 points—2 points each) Translate from French into English.

21.	des rois et des reines	
22.	un tambour et une tour	
23.	des tambours et des tours	
24.	un étudiant et une étudiante	
25.	des ducs et des duchesses	
26.	des étudiants et des étudiantes	

27.	une étudiante et un étudiant	
28.	un chat et une chatte	

PART 4

(16 points—2 points each) Translate from French into English.

29.	*Le roi et la reine pleuraient.*	
30.	*Le roi et la reine pleuraient-ils?*	
31.	*La reine chante.*	
32.	*Est-ce que la reine chante?*	
33.	*Le chat pleure-t-il?*	
34.	*La princesse chantait.*	
35.	*Est-ce que la princesse chantait?*	
36.	*La princesse chantait-elle?*	

PART 5

(14 points) Read the following story in English. Then read the same story in French and fill in the blanks with the words below. Answers can be used more than once.

This is a key. This is a king. And this is the king's kingdom. In this kingdom, there is a town. And in the town, there is a park. And in this park, there is a house. And in this house, there is a room. And in this room, there is a vase. And in this vase, there is a flower. Just imagine!

Clé	*fleur*	*maison*	*parc*	*pièce*
Roi	*royaume*	*vase*	*ville*	

Voici une 37._____ *Voici un* 38._____. *Et voici le royaume du roi. Dans ce* 39._____ *il y a une* 40._____ *Et dans ce* 41._____ *il y a un* 42._____ *Et dans ce* 43._____ *il y a une* 44._____ *Et dans cette* 45._____ *il y a une* 46._____ *Et dans cette* 47._____ *il y a un* 48._____. *Et dans cette* 49._____, *il y a une* 50._____ *Imaginez donc!*

PART 6

(9 points) Match the English phrases with the French equivalent.

51. _____ The queen is singing also. a. *Oui. Et ne chantent-ils pas bien?*
52. _____ Which queen? b. *Qui sait?*
53. _____ The one who was crying in the bathroom with the princess. c. *Oui. Elle chante dans la tour avec le roi.*
54. _____ The queen who was crying in the bathroom with the princess is singing? d. *Bien oui, il chantent plus ou moins bien. Mais pourquoi chantent-ils des chants funèbres?*
55. _____ Yes, she's singing in the tower with the king. e. *La reine chante aussi.*
56. _____ The king and queen are singing funeral chants in the tower? f. *Le roi et la reine chantent des chants funèbres dans la tour?*
57. _____ Yes. And don't they sing well? g. *Quelle reine?*
58. _____ Well yes, they sing more or less well. But why do they sing funeral chants? h. *Celle qui pleurait dans la salle de bains avec la princesse.*
59. _____ Who knows? i. *La reine qui pleurait dans la salle de bains avec la princesse chante?*

PART 7

(10 points) Write the correct numbers next to the word.

60. *dix mille dix* _____
61. *six mille six* _____
62. *neuf mille neuf cent* _____
63. *dix-neuf mille neuf cent* _____
64. *seize mille six cent six* _____
65. *dix-huit mille* _____
66. *neuf mille dix* _____
67. *dix-sept mille* _____
68. *trois mille neuf* _____
69. *seize mille* _____

PART 8

(15 points—3 points each) Translate from French into English.

70.	*D'où est Robert?*	
71.	*Est-ce qu'il est de Paris?*	
72.	*Qui est d'ici et qui est de Paris?*	
73.	*Le prince et la princesse sont ici.*	
74.	*Est-ce qu'ils sont ici?*	

French Test 3

Name _____
Total _____/100 points

PART 1

(15 points—3 points each) Read the story in French and then answer the questions below in English.

Voici une carte du monde. Le nord. Le sud. L'est. L'ouest. Voici le pôle nord, le pôle arctique. Voici le pôle sud, le pôle antarctique. La terre est notre vaisseau spatial. C'est une des neuf planètes qui tournent autour du soleil. C'est notre planète, notre maison. Sur la terre il y a deux hémisphères: Voici l'hémisphère nord. Voici l'hémisphère sud. Le noyau de la terre est extrêmement chaud. La plus grande partie de la surface de la terre est couverte d'eau. Il y a trois grands océans. L'océan Pacifique, l'océan Atlantique, et l'océan Indien. Voici l'océan Pacifique. C'est le plus grand océan. C'est également le plus profond. Il y a longtemps il y avait une seule grande masse de terre, mais maintenant elle est divisée en plusieurs continents. La plus grande masse de terre ou continent est ici. Elle s'étend de l'Europe à la Chine. Elle s'appelle l'Eurasie.

1. What is the largest land mass on earth?

2. What are the names of the hemisperes in the above passage?

3. What are the three oceans mentioned in the passage?

4. What is our "spaceship"?

5. How does this passage describe the center of the earth?

PART 2

(15 points) Match the English word with the French equivalent.

6.	_____	true	a.	*comment*
7.	_____	tonight	b.	*les deux*
8.	_____	how	c.	*maintenant*
9.	_____	when	d.	*encore*
10.	_____	both	e.	*déjà*
11.	_____	now	f.	*vrai*
12.	_____	often	g.	*formidable*
13.	_____	still	h.	*ce soir*
14.	_____	not yet	i.	*écouter*
15.	_____	already	j.	*vraiment*
16.	_____	where	k.	*ensemble*
17.	_____	to listen	l.	*quand*
18.	_____	great	m.	*souvent*
19.	_____	really	n.	*pas encore*
20.	_____	together	o.	*où*

PART 3

(15 points) Write the corresponding number next to the French word.

21. *cinquante-cinq* _____   29. *quatre-vingt-un* _____

22. *quatre-vingt-onze* _____   30. *soixante et onze* _____

23. *trente-trois* _____   31. *dix-neuf* _____

24. *vingt-six* _____   32. *douze* _____

25. *trente et un* _____   33. *quatorze* _____

26. *soixante-dix* _____   34. *mille vingt* _____

27. *quarante et un* _____   35. *deux mille* _____

28. *cinquante et un* _____

PART 4

(30 points—3 points each) Translate from French into English.

36.	*La princesse a menacé de chanter.*	
37.	*Le prince a décidé de manger le pain.*	
38.	*La prince a mangé le pain.*	
39.	*Le roi a commencé à parler.*	

40.	Le chat décide de jouer avec le chien.	
41.	La princesse menace de pleurer.	
42.	Elle promet de dire la vérité.	
43.	La reine commence à parler avec le roi.	
44.	Ils ont commencé à chanter.	
45.	Elle a décidé de commencer à chanter.	

PART 5
(10 points) Match the English word with the French translation.

46.	___	there	a.	se reposer
47.	___	to work	b.	être content
48.	___	to eat	c.	sans
49.	___	to be happy	d.	mais
50.	___	well	e.	dormir
51.	___	but	f.	là
52.	___	without	g.	manger
53.	___	to live	h.	vivre
54.	___	to sleep	i.	travailler
55.	___	to rest	j.	bien

PART 6
(15 points—3 points each) Translate from English into French.

56.	The prince has the drum.	
57.	The princes have the drums.	
58.	The dukes make the drums.	
59.	She doesn't have the cat.	
60.	They don't have the cat.	

French Test 1 Answers

PART 1 (7 POINTS)
1. the feet 2. the hands 3. the head 4. the face
5. the nose 6. an eye 7. the mouth

PART 2 (12 POINTS)
8. • 9. — 10. 1 11. • • —
12. — — — • • 3 13. 3 2 1 — —
14. • • • • — 2 15. — — — 3 4
16. 1 2 3 4 5 • • • • 17. • • • • — 18. — • • •
• • • 19. 1 2 3 4 5 6

PART 3 (11 POINTS)
20. c 21. d 22. g 23. h 24. f 25. i 26. a 27. e
28. k 29. b 30. j

PART 4 (15 POINTS)
31. *Un homme et une fille.* 32. *Marie est une fille.*
33. *Elle est une petite fille.* 34. *La mère et le père de Paul et Marie.* 35. *Il aime aider sa soeur.*

PART 5 (15 POINTS)
36. e 37. k 38. b 39. j 40. c 41. l 42. o 43. f
44. g 45. h 46. m 47. n 48. d 49. a 50. i

PART 6 (10 POINTS)
51. a 52. b 53. b 54. b 55. a 56. b 57. a 58. a
59. a 60. b

PART 7 (10 POINTS)
61. *quatre* 62. *cinq* 63. *six* 64. *six* 65. *dix* 66. *dix*
67. *deux* 68. *dix* 69. *mille* 70. *cent*

PART 8 (20 POINTS)
71. a 72. b 73. a 74. a 75. b 76. b 77. a 78. b
79. a 80. b 81. b 82. b 83. a 84. b 85. a 86. a
87. a 88. b 89. b 90. a

French Test 2 Answers

PART 1 (10 POINTS)
1. e 2. h 3. j 4. a 5. g 6. i 7. d 8. f 9. c 10. b

PART 2 (10 POINTS)
11. f 12. c 13. g 14. h 15. b 16. i 17. j 18. d
19. e 20. a

PART 3 (16 POINTS)
21. (some) kings and (some) queens 22. a drum and a tower 23. (some) drums and (some) towers 24. a male student and a female student 25. (some) dukes and (some) duchesses 26. (some) male students and (some) female students 27. a female student and a male student 28. a male cat and a female cat.

PART 4 (16 POINTS)
29. The king and the queen were crying. 30. Were the king and queen crying? 31. The queen is singing.
32. Is the queen singing? 33. Is the cat crying?
34. The princess used to sing. or The princess was singing. 35. Did the princess used to sing? or Was the princess singing? 36. Did the princess used to sing? or Was the princess singing?

PART 5 (14 POINTS)
37. *clé* 38. *roi* 39. *royaume* 40. *ville* 41. *ville*
42. *parc* 43. *parc* 44. *maison* 45. *maison* 46. *pièce*
47. *pièce* 48. *vase* 49. *vase* 50. *fleur*

PART 6 (9 POINTS)
51. e 52. g 53. h 54. i 55. c 56. f 57. a 58. d
59. b

PART 7 (10 POINTS)
60. 10,010 61. 6,006 62. 9,900 63. 19,900
64. 16,606 65. 18,000 66. 9,010 67. 17,000
68. 3,009 69. 16,000

PART 8 (15 POINTS)
70. Where is Robert from? 71. Is he from Paris?
72. Who is from here and who is from Paris? 73. The prince and the princess are here. 74. Are they here?

French Test 3 Answers

PART 1 (15 POINTS)
1. Eurasia 2. Northern and Southern Hemispheres
3. Pacific, Atlantic, and Indian 4. earth 5. very hot

PART 2 (15 POINTS)
6. f. 7. h. 8. a. 9. l. 10. b. 11. c. 12. m. 13. d.
14. n. 15. e. 16. o. 17. i. 18. g. 19. j. 20. k.

Part 3 (15 points)
21. 55 22. 91 23. 33 24. 26 25. 31 26. 70
27. 41 28. 51 29. 81 30. 71 31. 19 32. 12
33. 14 34. 1020 35. 2000

Part 4 (30 points)
36. The princess has threatened to sing. 37. The prince has decided to eat the bread. 38. The prince has eaten the bread. 39. The king has begun to speak. 40. The cat decides to play with the dog. 41. The princess threatens to cry. 42. She promises to tell the truth. 43. The queen begins to talk with the king. 44. They have begun to sing. 45. She has decided to begin to sing.

Part 5 (10 points)
46. f 47. i 48. g 49. b 50. j 51. d 52. c 53. h
54. e 55. a.

Part 6 (15 points)
56. Le prince a le tambour. 57. Les princes ont les tambours. 58. Les ducs font les tambours. 59. Elle n'a pas le chat. 60. Ils n'ont pas le chat

French 1, Semester 2

I hope you realize how much you can do with your language. Let's begin. Semester 2 is broken up into 3 sections just like semester 1.

Section 1

After completing this section you will be able to:

- Identify and say various shapes, geometrical or otherwise.
- Comprehend the meaning of stories and lectures.
- Use new vocabulary to create your own spontaneous conversations.
- Learn new geography vocabulary.
- Describe body parts in more complex sentences.
- Read for meaning.
- Retell stories without memorization.
- Interact in a classroom setting.
- Use problem-solving techniques with multiple-choice frames.
- Build grammar and speaking fluency.
- Use past, present, and future tense.
- Pronounce the consonants in French with an improved accent.
- String together your own narratives.
- Use cardinals and ordinals in French.
- Use immediate and extended family vocabulary.
- Expand cultural knowledge of French speaking countries.

☐ Lesson 1-1

Turn to activity #43. Look over these new points, lines, and figures. As you do each section of this activity, remember that as you perform the functions, your brain is retaining and processing the information you are learning. The multiple-choice

Journal/Notes:

frames help you develop problem-solving techniques in French.

☐ **1-2**

Turn to activity #44. This is a new story. Read both the English and the French. Listen to the French while you read along. Make sure you know all the words for the picture prompts. Read through and listen to the story as many times as necessary. Remember, you don't have to memorize the story. Use the pictures to help key your memory. Tell the story to at least two different audiences.

☐ **1-3**

Activity #45 is another geography lesson. Cover the English and listen to the French audio as if you were really in a French geography class. How many new vocabulary words can you pick up? Can you say all of the continents in French? Pretend you are the teacher. How much of the geography lesson can you give to another person? When you're finished telling at least two people what you learned move to the next activity.

☐ **1-4**

Activity #46 is a simulation of a mother talking with her child. Listen as the mother not only identifies body parts, but describes them as well and then makes associations to things the child can understand. Before you finish this activity, find a child and see how many descriptions and associations you can make with body part vocabulary.

Journal/Notes:

Make sure you read the rest of the adventure before moving to activity #47.

☐ **1-5**

Turn to activity #47 in your workbook. You've done an activity like this before so you may want to collect a few physical objects before you continue. Listen carefully to know what to say with each object. Try to teach the main idea to another person.

☐ **1-6**

It's time for another adventure with La Mouche! Go to the CD-ROM and pick up where you left off last. Focus on comprehending the language and see if you can say some things in French just like La Mouche.

☐ **1-7**

Turn to activity #48. Here are some more points, lines, and figures. Spend plenty of time focusing on the names for each shape in French. Go through each section of the activity and work toward full comprehension. If you make a mistake, that means you're still learning. Each step is a learning process. Know that you can be successful.

☐ **1-8**

Turn to activity #49. This activity is done without the audio. Go over each pictograph and its French equivalent. Say each word aloud to hear your pronunciation. Say each sentence, focusing on the French sentence construction. You may be tempted to write the English equivalents down, but resist that temptation and you will produce more fluent French.

☐ **1-9**

Turn to activity #50 and read part 2 of the diglot-weave, "My First Visit to Quebec." Focus on using the new vocabulary. Give a summary of this story in French to at least 2 different people.

☐ **1-10**

Turn to activity #51 and read a lecture on the French alphabet. Work on the pronunciation of the consonant sound with the speakers on the audio. Work toward understanding the French meaning of this activity and don't focus on figuring out the English translation.

☐ **1-11**

Turn to activity #52 and work on creating your own sentences. Make sure you are familiar with the words in the scatter chart and the sentence structures in the examples before you create your own sentences. Note the reasons some of the sentences may not be grammatically correct. Try to remember the rules and this will improve your own sentences. Create 15 or more of your own sentences. Say them aloud and write them down.

☐ **1-12**

Turn again to activity #53. This activity will help you use French vocabulary in your math class. Learn what cardinal and ordinal numbers are in French. This activity reviews your numbers so do something fun to help you review. Challenge: create a math problem using the numbers on this page and teach it (in French) to another person.

☐ **1-13**

Activity #54 is another activity that focuses on grammar. Read through the rules and examples. Say each example until you don't hesitate, and try writing them as well to improve your writing skills. When you complete each grammar focus, move on.

☐ **1-14**

Activity #55 is designed to help you build fluency in your sentence patterns. Add the vocabulary in the scatter chart to your vocabulary base. Translate the sentences and then create an activity that is similar using your own thoughts in French. You may want to use this type of activity for one of your portfolio projects.

☐ **1-15**

Activity #56 has some easy but very important vocabulary. It's important in some cultures that you know how to talk about both your immediate and extended family. Incorporating the words from

Journal/Notes:

this activity will help you discuss your immediate as well as extended family. Do each exercise of the activity and then create some type of introduction about your own family. This will help you solidify your knowledge. Read the adventure and cultural overview of Luxembourg.

☐ **1-16**

Do additional research on Luxembourg on the web site. Remember that you need to write one research paper per semester to receive credit, and you might want to use this time to research a country of your choice or begin to put your thoughts together for your paper. You have the entire semester to work on it, and you don't have to write it all at once. Remember to plan carefully and make time to write at least a rough and final draft. Put all your notes and work in your academic portfolio file.

☐ **1-17**

You are now ready to take progress test #4. Review grammar and any vocabulary learned in this section. You will know you are ready when you can meet the objectives for this section as well as understand vocabulary and grammar.

☐ **1-18**

Take progress test #4. Go to http://www.power-glide.com/progresstests and take test #4. When you receive your results, review the errors and when you feel comfortable with how to correct those errors, take written test #4.

☐ **1-19**

Take written test #4. Have it corrected and put the results in your academic portfolio file.

Section 2

How can learning French help you on your adventure through learning? Let's begin and find out!

After completing this section you will be able to:
- Focus and use action words.
- Build fluency in French grammar patterns and speech.
- Use geography vocabulary.
- Understand a French proverb.
- Understand and perform instructions given.
- Make complex descriptions.
- Learn and use infinitives and interrogatives.
- Review sentence patterns with targeted vocabulary
- Test your performance and make assumptions of your progress.
- Create and tell stories.
- Word toward perfection in pronouncing the French alphabet.

Journal/Notes:

- Ask and answer very simple questions.
- Expand listening and reading comprehension.

☐ Lesson 2-1

Turn to activity #57. Learn the pictures for the various actions and practice them aloud. You may want to spend time creating your own match and learn activity until you really know each one of the actions in French. When you know each word well, finish each section of the activity. Don't shortcut yourself on activity F, even if you feel a little awkward doing it. Try to make a game of it. Before moving to the next activity, try to make some of your own sentences using these action words.

☐ 2-2

Turn to activity #58 and work through another series of pictograph sentences without the audio. Say everything aloud. If you've been recording yourself, this might be a good time to compare your speaking skills now to what they were when you started. Are they improving? You can tell you're improving if you have fewer hesitations between words, and if the French sounds natural and not monotone. You may detect errors in your speech. This is great because it means you can comprehend the grammar rules even if you can't articulate them.

☐ 2-3

Open your workbook to activity #59. It's time for some more geography. Get out your map and label the locations discussed in this geography lesson. In French, tell at least two different people what you learned in this activity and show them the map. (You can make a map or you can use a globe or anything else you have. Try to make a connection by using a physical object when learning new vocabulary.)

☐ 2-4

Activity #60 is a French proverb. Read it through and work toward understanding the entire proverb in French before looking at the translation. What is the message? Can you articulate it? Don't spend time memorizing this text; work toward repeating its message. You will have another chance at this later.

☐ 2-5

For activity #61 gather a regular pencil, a red pencil, a sheet of white paper, and a sheet of red paper, a box, and a sack. Cover up the English translation. Listen to the French audio and try to perform the instructions as they are given. Repeat the activity until you can complete most of the instructions. Using the same sentences structures, give instructions to another person and see if they can follow them.

☐ 2-6

Turn to activity #62. Read through both the English and the French. Listen to the audio and read through the French again. Notice how the descriptions the mother is giving to the child

Journal/Notes:

become more complex. Notice how associations are made with the descriptions. Find two storybooks in your house and see if you can go through them and make descriptions of the characters patterned after the stories in this activity. Practice describing one or two characters to another person in French. It doesn't matter if the other person speaks French or not; they will learn something new.

☐ 2-7 ☐ 🔊

Young children are very inquisitive. If you stop and listen to them, you'll find that they ask a million different kinds of questions. Turn to activity #63 and learn some of the questions children ask their parents. Ask similar questions on your level. See how many you can ask your family during dinner!

☐ 2-8 ☐

Open to your workbook to activity #64 and learn this short conversation. This is done without audio so say everything aloud in French as you read it. Can you make your own similar conversation and share it with another person? Try to make opportunities to use your language skills outside of the study session before moving to another activity.

☐ 2-9 ☐

Let's focus on some more grammar and put it to good use. Turn to activity #65 and read each grammar explanation and say the examples aloud. When you're translating, do both oral and written translations. Review why certain sentence patterns are not what you think they may be. Concentrate on how the French put words together.

☐ 2-10 ☐

Activity #66 is a review of different sentence patterns. Most of the vocabulary comes from "Chatter at the Royal Ball" activities. These activities are designed to push you into thinking in the target language. Focus more on the French sentences than the English sentences. When you feel like you understand each group of sentences move to the next activity.

☐ 2-11 ☐

Activity #67 is similar to the previous activity. This time you are concentrating on the English sentences and how to say the French. There are two thought processes when you study a foreign language. One is you think of something to say in your native language and then translate it into the target language. The other is actually forming thoughts in the target language and never thinking about it in your native language. Each process is important to your language acquisition. Remember not to be frustrated if you don't get everything correct in your translations. Keep moving forward.

☐ 2-12 ☐

How do you feel about your comprehension? Can you identify your own progress? Read activity #68 and answer the questions. This will help you evaluate how you're progressing in your comprehen-

Journal/Notes:

. . . .

. . . .

. . . .

. . . .

. . . .

sion. If you can answer all the questions correctly without hesitation you are doing superbly. If you struggle than you are probably more like the rest of us who may need to read the text several times in order to answer the questions. Either way you're moving forward.

☐ **2-13**

Creating your own sentences and stories helps you build fluency in French. Turn to activity #69 and review the parts of speech that make your sentences have variety. Do the sentence-construction exercise and then stop.

☐ **2-14**

Turn to activity #69 again and read about how to construct stories and read the sample story. Use the guidelines to write your own story. Gather ideas and write out a rough draft. Leave the rough draft alone and go do an adventure with La Mouche or another fun activity for at least one study session.

☐ **2-15**

Resume activity #69 by reading through your rough draft. Does it make sense? Can you detect any errors? Do you need to add anything? Subtract anything? Write your final draft and then practice reading it aloud. Tell your story to another person, but don't just read it. It will be more interesting if you can tell the story—it won't sound so monotone. You may want to do this activity for one of your portfolio projects.

Journal/Notes:

☐ **2-16**

Turn to activity #70 and work your French pronunciation and alphabet. There isn't an English translation so focus hard on the French. If there are words you can't understand from context, use the CD-ROM dictionary to discover their meanings.

☐ **2-17**

Activity #71 is another example of simple questions a child might ask. How many questions can you ask that are of interest to you? Follow these simple patterns and come up with a few. Ask another French speaker and see if they can answer your questions.

☐ **2-18**

Turn to activity #72. Listen to the story and learn some new vocabulary. Use your new vocabulary in at least 10 different sentences to help you remember them. You can do this by retelling the story or creating a new one of your own using the same vocabulary. If you create a new story, you may want to use it for a portfolio project.

☐ **2-19**

Turn to activity #73 in your workbook. You need to pretend you are in a French only classroom again. The geography discussed in this lesson will help you understand the French names for the countries of Europe and Asia. Go to the web site, http://www.power-glide.com/french/links and click on the French newspaper link. Can you read anything about one of the countries you studied? If this isn't an option use your local newspaper and find out something about one of the countries in this activity and explain it in French. This may be a challenge but it will be good practice. Always look for opportunities to use your language.

☐ 2-20

Turn to activity #74 and learn to tell a simplified version of "The Three Pigs." Learn the story and then tell it to another person. You may want to make visuals to help you remember the main points of the story. You will be doing this story again, so don't throw your visuals away.

☐ 2-21

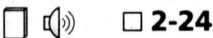

Activity #75 is part 3 of "My First Visit to Quebec." You may want to review part 1 and part 2 of the story in order to remember vocabulary. Focus on the meaning. Then try to tell someone else what the trip was like. Use as many study sessions as you need to comprehend this story.

☐ 2-22

It's time to prepare for progress test #5. Review self-tests, vocabulary, grammar rules, and anything else you feel you need work on. Make sure you are confident with the material before taking the test.

☐ 2-23

Take the online progress test #5. Go to http://www.power-glide.com/progresstests and fill in your name and e-mail address. Review your test when you receive it and go over any errors that you may have. Research how to correct those errors by going back to the sections of the workbook in this section.

☐ 2-24

Take written test #5. Have it corrected and put the results in your academic portfolio file for evaluation.

Section 3

You're almost done with French 1! Did you ever think you could learn so much in such a small amount of time? Amazing isn't it? Let's begin right away.

After completing this section you will be able to:
- Ask and answer questions in French.
- Use action verbs in a sentence.
- Read and use geography vocabulary.

Journal/Notes:

- Learn new vocabulary through readings and stories in French.
- Act out what you've read.
- Compose new sentences orally and in writing.
- Use adjective-noun gender agreement.
- Use possessive pronouns correctly.
- Identify pictures from a description
- Expand culture knowledge.
- Learn to use humor in your conversations.

☐ Lesson 3-1

Let's begin this section with more pictographs. Turn to activity #76. Learn the new words and pictographs in the scatter chart and begin to make associations that will help you remember the pictures. Complete each section until you can produce comprehension, spelling, or speaking without a great deal of hesitation.

☐ 3-2

Turn to activity #77 for another geography lesson in French. Cover the English text and work toward comprehension in French. Write down your own English translation and check it against the written English text. If your translations are similar in meaning, even without using the same words, you know you are progressing.

☐ 3-3

Activity #78 is a short story to help you work toward full French comprehension. Read both texts and then cover the English. Translate from French to English and English to French. Tell someone about what you did in this study session. Continue with the adventure and collect all the clues you can.

☐ 3-4

Activity #79 is another French lesson using pencil and paper. Follow the instructions given for this activity. Use real objects to teach this lesson to another person as if you were the teacher on the audio. Work toward teaching the same concepts without hesitation. If you make a mistake, it's okay. It's better to make a mistake and produce speech than it is to wait around until it comes out perfect and produce nothing.

☐ 3-5

Let's use your imagination to continue to build your thinking and speaking skills in French. Turn to activity #80 and work with the "Royal" family. What kinds of sentence patterns can you use from this lesson? Look for ways to use the same sentence patterns in your own speech. Use your imagination to create a story or conversation using the new vocabulary and grammar given in this lesson.

☐ 3-6

It's time for another grammar focus. Turn to activity #81 and work on adjective-noun gender agreement, possessive pronouns, and understanding how to use new verbs. Work over each section until you can produce at least 2 or 3 of your own sentences without looking.

Journal/Notes:

☐ 3-7

After an intensive grammar review go to the CD-ROM and have a fun adventure with La Mouche. Use this time to recognize how much you can comprehend French in a different setting? Can you think in French as you listen to the French speakers on the audio? Can you formulate your own questions in French like La Mouche? Try to make a conscious effort to realize your progress.

☐ 3-8

It's amazing how much a small child can learn from just a few exposures to new situations. Turn to activity #82 and pretend you are a small child at the zoo. Listen to the questions the child asks and how they are answered. Formulate some of your own questions and then pretend you are the adult and answer them. The more questions and answers you can come up with, the more you will remember and improve your own skills.

☐ 3-9

Turn to activity #83 and read through this short conversation. Again you are focusing on how a child learns to communicate with an adult. Formulate some French questions you might ask if you were a child. Answer those same questions as the adult. Which one is more difficult? Do you need to simplify your French answers? Learn to focus on the words and phrases you can say so that you can communicate even if it is simplified.

☐ 3-10

The next two activities will appeal to those of you who tell jokes with puns. Turn to activity #84 and #85. Read through both the English and French. Listen to the French audio as many times as necessary in order to retell the jokes without hesitancy. Try to perform the joke without sounding like you've memorized it. (A memorized joke lacks the appropriate intonations and the listener might miss the pun.)

☐ 3-11

Turn to activity #86 and read part 4 of "My First Visit to Quebec." You may want to review the vocabulary in the other segments in order to refresh your memory. (Activity #38, #50, and #75) This segment is rather long, so allow yourself plenty of study sessions to comprehend the new information.

☐ 3-12

Go to the CD-ROM and take another adventure with La Mouche. These adventures are not only fun but they help you recognize the growth of your comprehension skills.

☐ 3-13

Turn to activity #87 and use the scatter chart as an aid to developing new conversations. Read the samples and then come up with your own version using your creativity. The more sentences you can

Journal/Notes:

create on your own, the more spontaneous your own conversations will be.

☐ 3-14

You are now ready for progress test #6. Can you believe you've completed a year's worth of study? Do you feel comfortable with the new information you learned in this section? Are you able to meet the objectives? In order to prepare for the progress as well as the written test review grammar focus activities, vocabulary, comprehension activities and anything else you feel you need to work on.

☐ 3-15

Take progress test #6? Go to http://www.power-glide.com/progresstests and fill in your name and e-mail address. When you receive your results find your errors, if you have any, and review the information carefully so you can do well on the written test.

☐ 3-16

Take written test #6. Have it corrected and put the results in your academic portfolio file.

> *If you are seeking credit for this course, review the "How to Receive Credi t" information in the Overview at the beginning of this Guide. You will need to have a completed portfolio according to the specifications in the Overview.*

Journal/Notes:

- -

- -

- -

- -

- -

French Test 4

Name _____
Total _____/100 points

PART 1

(30 points) Read the following story in English. Then read the same story in French and fill in the blanks with the words provided. Answers may be used more than once.

Here is your little girl dolly. Her name is Ann. Ann has hands and feet. Her hands and feet are like yours. But they are very little. Look how little they are. Two little tiny hands. Here is your little boy dolly. His name is Pinocchio. He is Ann's big brother. Does Pinocchio have hands and feet? He has hands and feet like Ann's. He has hands and feet just like yours. Look, his head and feet are like yours. Does Pinnochio have a nose? Yes, look at his nose. He has a long nose. Is his nose like Ann's? No, Pinocchio's nose is long.

celui	très	comme	des	deux
exactement	frère	grand	long	mains
minuscules	nez	petite	pieds	poupée
poupon	regarde	s'appelle	ton	

Voici ta 1._____ 2._____. *Elle* 3._____ *Anne. Anne a* 4._____ 5._____ *et des* 6._____. *Ses* 7._____ *et ses* 8._____ *sont* 9._____ *les tiens. Mais ils sont* 10._____ *petits.* 11._____ *comme ils sont petits.* 12._____ *petites* 13._____ 14._____. *Voici* 15._____ *petit* 16._____. *Il* 17._____ *Pinocchio. C'est le* 18._____ 19._____ *d'Anne. Est-ce que Pinocchio a* 20._____ 21._____ *et* 22._____ 23._____ *? Il a des mains et des pieds comme ceux d'Anne. Il a des mains et des pieds* 24._____ *comme toi. Regarde, ses mains et ses pieds sont* 25._____ *les tiens. Est-ce que Pinocchio a un nez? Oui, regarde son nez. Il a un long nez. Est-ce que son* 26._____ *est* 27._____ 28._____ *d'Anne? Non, le* 29._____ *de Pinocchio est* 30._____.

PART 2

(10 points) Write the English translation next to the French sentence.

31.	*Voici les clés de Rome.*	
32.	*La dame n'est pas dans le lit.*	
33.	*La place n'est pas à Rome.*	
34.	*Ce continent-ci est l'Afrique.*	
35.	*Le Brésil est un très grand pays.*	

36.	C'est l'Amérique du Sud.	
37.	Au nord de l'Afrique se trouve l'Egypte.	
38.	L'Amazone coule vers l'est à travers le Brésil.	
39.	C'est la plus grande rivière du monde.	
40.	Il y a beaucoup de serpents et de reptiles.	

PART 3

(20 points) Write the French equivalent next to the English number.

41. one _____   51. eleven _____

42. two _____   52. twelve _____

43. three _____   53. thirteen _____

44. four _____   54. fourteen _____

45. five _____   55. fifteen _____

46. six _____   56. sixteen _____

47. seven _____   57. seventeen _____

48. eight _____   58. eighteen _____

49. nine _____   59. nineteen _____

50. ten _____   60. twenty _____

PART 4

(10 points) Write the French equivalent next to the English number.

61. thirty _____   66. eighty _____

62. forty _____   67. ninety _____

63. fifty _____   68. one hundred _____

64. sixty _____   69. one hundred and one _____

65. seventy _____   70. one thousand _____

PART 5
(15 points) Match the English word with the French translation.

71.	____	give	a.	*petite*
72.	____	take	b.	*toute(s)*
73.	____	there	c.	*autre*
74.	____	also	d.	*prenez*
75.	____	black	e.	*moi*
76.	____	white	f.	*là-bas*
77.	____	not	g.	*donnez*
78.	____	me	h.	*ne, n'...pas*
79.	____	other	i.	*blanche*
80.	____	long	j.	*il y a*
81.	____	lying down	k.	*tige*
82.	____	rod	l.	*longue*
83.	____	there is	m.	*aussi*
84.	____	small	n.	*couchée*
85.	____	all	o.	*noir*

PART 6
(15 points) Translate the French sentences into English.

86.	*Elle ne chante que dans la tour.*	
87.	*Et elle ne chante qu'un peu dans la tour.*	
88.	*Elle ne chante qu'avec le prince.*	
89.	*Elle ne chante que des chants funèbres.*	
90.	*Elle n'a que deux chats.*	
91.	*Il n'a qu'un chat.*	
92.	*Le prince n'a qu'un chien.*	
93.	*Le roi ne fait que chanter.*	
94.	*Il ne boit jamais.*	
95.	*Il ne boit rien.*	
96.	*Il ne boit pas de lait.*	
97.	*Elle ne chante jamais à l'école.*	
98.	*Je ne sais pas.*	
99.	*Je n'en sais rien.*	
100.	*Ce n'est rien.*	

French Test 5

Name _____
Total _____ /100 points

PART 1
(20 points—2 points each) Translate from English into French.

1.	James has a long, black beard.	
2.	This is a baby.	
3.	Smee is a pirate.	
4.	Does Captain Hook have friends?	
5.	Without eyes, you (*tu* form) can't see anything.	
6.	Do you (*tu* form) know why he only has one arm?	
7.	It's because a crocodile ate the other.	
8.	He has only one eye.	
9.	Some babies don't have hair.	
10.	He doesn't have friends.	

PART 2
(20 points—2 points each) Translate from French into English.

11.	*Voici un vilain géant, un monstre.*	
12.	*Il est né avec un seul oeil.*	
13.	*Au moins il peut voir.*	
14.	*Il n'est pas aveugle.*	
15.	*Mais il n'a pas d'amis.*	
16.	*Pourquoi n'a-t-il pas d'amis?*	
17.	*Parce que les gens n'aiment pas les monstres qui n'ont qu'un oeil au milieu de leur front.*	
18.	*Ils ont peur d'eux.*	

| 19. | *Il déteste tout le monde.* | |
| 20. | *Je crois qu'il se déteste lui-même.* | |

PART 3

(20 points) Match the English phrase with the French translation.

21.	____	there is/are	a.	*vraiment*
22.	____	to ask	b.	*le poète de la cour*
23.	____	to live	c.	*la jolie secrétaire*
24.	____	to dwell	d.	*lequel*
25.	____	what is more	e.	*le jardinier*
26.	____	naturally, of course	f.	*il y a*
27.	____	truly, really	g.	*lesquels*
28.	____	which one	h.	*le juge impartial*
29.	____	which ones	i.	*demander*
30.	____	here it is	j.	*le voici*
31.	____	here they are	k.	*le magicien de la cour*
32.	____	this one	l.	*vivre*
33.	____	that one	m.	*les voici*
34.	____	scandalous	n.	*la femme de chambre*
35.	____	the court poet	o.	*habiter*
36.	____	the pretty secretary	p.	*ceci, celui-ci*
37.	____	the gardener	q.	*cela, celui-la*
38.	____	the impartial judge	r.	*qui plus est*
39.	____	the court magician	s.	*scandaleux*
40.	____	the chambermaid	t.	*naturellement*

PART 4

(20 points) Translate from French into English.

41.	*Trois petits cochons.*	
42.	*Frères.*	
43.	*Trois maisons.*	
44.	*Une maison en paille.*	
45.	*Une maison en planches.*	
46.	*Une maison en briques.*	
47.	*Un loup.*	
48.	*Il vient affamé.*	
49.	*Il vient à la maison en paille.*	
50.	*Il souffle.*	

51.	La maison en paille tombe.	
52.	Le loup vient une fois de plus.	
53.	Il vient à la maison en planches.	
54.	Mais le petit cochon s'échappe.	
55.	Il vient à la maison en briques.	
56.	Il est très affamé.	
57.	Il souffle une fois de plus.	
58.	Mais la maison en briques ne tombe pas.	
59.	Et le loup part.	
60.	Très, très affamé.	

PART 5

(20 points) Read the following story in English. Then read the same story in French and fill in the blanks with the words below. Answers can be used more than once.

Between South America and North America lies Central America. Panama is here. In Panama, there is a canal that links the Atlantic and the Pacific Oceans. The canal is a bridge between east and west. Farther north lies Mexico. Its capital is Mexico City. It is destined to become the world's largest city. North of Mexico is the United States. The U.S. lies between the Pacific and the Atlantic oceans. The east coast touches the Atlantic. The south coast touches the Gulf of Mexico. The capital, Washington D.C., is on the east coast. The largest city, New York, is there too.

aussi	canal	capitale	centrale
destinée	entre	grande	joint
l'ouest	nord	Pacifique	plus
plus	pont	s'étendent	sud
touche	trouve	ville	

61._____ l'Amérique du sud et l'Amérique du 62._____ se trouve l'Amérique 63._____. Panama se trouve là. A Panama il y a un 64._____ qui 65._____ l'océan Atlantique à l'océan 66._____. Le canal est un 67._____ entre l'est et 68._____. 69._____ au nord se trouve le Mexique. Sa 70._____ est Mexico. Elle est 71._____ à devenir la plus grande 72._____ du monde. Au nord du Mexique se trouvent les Etats-Unis. Les Etats-Unis 73._____ entre l'océan Pacifique et l'océan Atlantique. La côte est 74._____ l'Atlantique. La côte 75._____ 76._____ le Golfe du Mexique. La capitale, Washington D.C., se trouve sur la côte est. La 77._____ 78._____ ville, New York, s'y 79._____ 80._____.

French Test 6

Name _____
Total _____ /100 points

Part 1

(20 points) Read the following story in English. Then read the same story in French and fill in the blanks with the words below. Answers can be used more than once.

This picture represents the solar system. In orbit around the sun there are nine planets. We live on one of those planets, the third from the sun. We call our planet: Earth. Like all other planets, our earth is a satellite from the sun. It orbits the sun once every year. The earth has its own satellite. It is called the moon. The moon orbits the earth about once every month, or rather about once every 28 days. The earth has two poles: the north pole and the south pole delimitated by two circles, Arctic and Antarctic. The earth is divided into two hemispheres: the northern and southern hemispheres.

autour	cercles	deux	jours	lune
mois	neuf	Nord	pôle	satellite
solaire	soleil	Sud	terre	troisième

Ce dessin représente le système 1._____. En orbite autour du soleil il y a 2._____ planètes. Nous vivons sur l'une de ces planètes, la 3._____ du 4._____. Nous appelons notre planète: 5._____. Comme toutes les autres planètes, notre terre est un 6._____ du 7._____. Elle tourne 8._____ du 9._____ une fois par an. La terre a son propre satellite. Il s'appelle la 10._____. La 11._____ tourne autour de la 12._____ environ une fois par 13._____, ou plutôt environ une fois tous les 28 14._____. La terre a deux pôles, le 15._____ Nord et le 16._____ 17._____ délimités par deux 18._____ pôlaires, Nord et Sud. La terre est divisée en 19._____ hémisphères: l'hémisphère 20._____ et l'hémisphère Sud.

Part 2

(10 points) Translate the English phrases into French. Use the *vous* form when applicable.

21.	This is my pencil.	
22.	It's mine.	
23.	This pencil is mine.	
24.	Your pencil is long.	

25.	But this pencil is short.	
26.	Your paper is here.	
27.	That paper is small.	
28.	I believe it's yours.	
29.	This is your pencil.	
30.	Thank you.	

PART 3

(30 points—2 points each) Match the English word with the French translation.

31.	_____	to eat butter	a.	*couvrir*
32.	_____	to delude, deceive	b.	*gros, grosse*
33.	_____	to deceive oneself	c.	*alors*
34.	_____	to ask	d.	*heureux, heureuse*
35.	_____	to wonder	e.	*de la crème de lait*
36.	_____	to cover	f.	*malheureusement*
37.	_____	happy	g.	*manger du beurre*
38.	_____	unfortunately	h.	*partout*
39.	_____	usually	i.	*tromper*
40.	_____	he himself	j.	*d'habitude*
41.	_____	fat	k.	*se tromper*
42.	_____	then	l.	*au moins*
43.	_____	some cream from milk	m.	*demander*
44.	_____	everywhere	n.	*lui même*
45.	_____	at least	o.	*se demander*

PART 4

(20 points—2 points each) Translate from French into English.

46.	*Le gros fils chante.*	
47.	*La grosse fille joue.*	
48.	*Le père est gros.*	
49.	*La mère n'est pas grosse.*	
50.	*Il est bon et elle est bonne.*	
51.	*Le beau duc ne danse jamais.*	
52.	*La belle duchesse non plus.*	
53.	*Le bon roi est content.*	

54.	*Et la bonne reine est contente aussi.*	
55.	*La bonne duchesse est ici.*	

PART 5

(20 points—2 points each) Place the French sentences in the correct word order.

56.	I wonder if she loves the prince.	*aime demande elle je le me prince. si*	
57.	I wonder if she remembers me.	*de demande elle me moi. se si souvient je*	
58.	If I am not mistaken, he is a duke.	*duc. est il je me ne pas, si trompe un*	
59.	Unfortunately, they are mistaken.	*ils malheureusement, se trompent.*	
60.	Kings talk a lot.	*beaucoup. les parlent rois*	
61.	Princes eat a lot of ice cream.	*beaucoup de glace. les mangent princes*	
62.	What do kings do?	*font-ils? les que rois,*	
63.	Dogs and cats can dance.	*chats chiens danser. et les les peuvent*	
64.	The rich are the same everywhere.	*les les mêmes. partout riches sont*	
65.	What do cats eat?	*chats, ils? les mangent que*	

French Test 4 Answers

PART 1 (30 POINTS)
1. *petite* 2. *poupée* 3. *s'appelle* 4. *des* 5. *mains*
6. *pieds* 7. *mains* 8. *pieds* 9. *comme* 10. *très*
11. *regarde* 12. *deux* 13. *mains* 14. *minuscules*
15. *ton* 16. *poupon* 17. *s'appelle* 18. *grand*
19. *frère* 20. *des* 21. *mains* 22. *des* 23. *pieds*
24. *exactement* 25. *comme* 26. *nez* 27. *comme*
28. *celui* 29. *nez* 30. *long.*

PART 2 (10 POINTS)
31. Here are the keys to Rome. 32. The lady isn't in the bed. 33. The plaza isn't in Rome. 34. This continent here is Africa. 35. Brazil is a very large country. 36. This is South America. 37. In the northern part of Africa is Egypt. 38. The Amazon flows east through Brazil. 39. It is the largest river in the world. 40. There are many snakes and reptiles.

PART 3 (20 POINTS)
41. *un* 42. *deux* 43. *trois* 44. *quatre* 45. *cinq*
46. *six* 47. *sept* 48. *huit* 49. *neuf* 50. *dix*
51. *onze* 52. *douze* 53. *treize* 54. *quatorze*
55. *quinze* 56. *seize* 57. *dix-sept* 58. *dix-huit*
59. *dix-neuf* 60. *vingt*

PART 4 (10 POINTS)
61. *trente* 62. *quarante* 63. *cinquante* 64. *soixante*
65. *soixante-dix* 66. *quatre-vingt* 67. *quatre-vingt-dix*
68. *cent* 69. *cent un* 70. *mille*

PART 5 (15 POINTS)
71. g. 72. d. 73. f. 74. m. 75. o. 76. i. 77. h.
78. e. 79. c. 80. l. 81. n. 82. k. 83. j. 84. a.
85. b.

PART 6 (15 POINTS)
86. She sings only in the tower. 87. And she sings only a little in the tower. 88. She sings only with the prince. 89. She doesn't sing anything but funeral chants. 90. She has only two cats. 91. He doesn't have but one cat. 92. The prince has but one dog. 93. The king does nothing but sing. 94. He never drinks. 95. He drinks nothing. 96. He doesn't drink milk. 97. She never sings at school. 98. I don't know. 99. I know nothing about it. 100. That's nothing.

French Test 5 Answers

PART 1 (20 POINTS)
1. *Jacques a une longue barbe noire.* 2. *Ceci est un bébé.* 3. *Smee est un pirate.* 4. *Est-ce que Capitaine Crochet a des amis?* 5. *Sans yeux tu ne peux rien voir.* 6. *Sais-tu pourquoi il n'a qu'un bras?* 7. *C'est parce qu'un crocodile a mangé l'autre.* 8. *Il n'a qu'un oeil.* 9. *Certains bébés n'ont pas de cheveux.* 10. *Il n'a pas d'amis.*

PART 2 (20 POINTS)
11. Here is an ugly giant, a monster. 12. He was born with only one eye. 13. At least he can see. 14. He is not blind. 15. But he doesn't have any friends. 16. Why doesn't he have any friends? 17. Because people don't like monsters with only one eye in the middle of their forehead. 18. They are afraid of them. 19. He hates everyone. 20. I think he even hates himself.

PART 3 (20 POINTS)
21. f 22. i. 23. l. 24. o. 25. r. 26. t. 27. a.
28. d. 29. g. 30. j. 31. m. 32. p. 33. q. 34. s.
35. b. 36. c. 37. e. 38. h. 39. k. 40. n.

PART 4 (20 POINTS)
41. Three little pigs. 42. Brothers. 43. Three houses. 44. A house of straw. 45. A house of sticks. 46. A house of bricks. 47. A wolf. 48. He comes hungry. 49. He comes to the house of straw. 50. He blows. 51. The house of straw falls. 52. The wolf comes another time. 53. He comes to the house of sticks. 54. But the little pig escapes. 55. He comes to the house of bricks. 56. He is very hungry. 57. He blows another time. 58. But the house of bricks doesn't fall. 59. And the wolf leaves. 60. Very, very hungry.

PART 5 (20 POINTS)
61. *entre* 62. *nord* 63. *centrale* 64. *canal* 65. *joint*
66. *Pacifique* 67. *pont* 68 *l'ouest* 69. *plus*
70. *capitale* 71. *destinée* 72. *ville* 73. *s'étendent*
74. *touche* 75. *sud* 76. *touche* 77. *plus* 78. *grande*
79. *trouve* 80. *aussi*

French Test 6 Answers

Part 1 (20 points)
1. *solaire* 2. *neuf* 3. *troisième* 4. *soleil* 5. *terre*
6. *satellite* 7. *soleil* 8. *autour* 9. *soleil* 10. *lune*
11. *lune* 12. *terre* 13. *mois* 14. *jours* 15. *pôle*
16. *pôle* 17. *sud* 18. *cercles* 19. *deux* 20. *nord*

Part 2 (10 points)
21. *C'est mon crayon.* 22. *C'est le mien.* 23. *Ce crayon est le mien.* 24. *Votre crayon est long.*
25. *Mais ce crayon est petit.* 26. *Votre papier est ici.*
27. *Ce papier est petit.* 28. *Je crois que c'est le vôtre.*
29. *Ceci est votre crayon.* 30. *Merci.*

Part 3 (30 points)
31. g. 32. i. 33. k. 34. m. 35. o 36. a. 37. d.
38. f. 39. j. 40. n. 41. b. 42. c. 43. e. 44. h.
45. l.

Part 4 (20 points)
46. The fat son sings. 47. The fat daughter plays.
48. The father is fat. 49. The mother is not fat.
50. He is good and she is good. 51. The handsome duke doesn't ever dance. 52. The beautiful duchess doesn't either. 53. The good king is content. 54. And the good queen is content, too. 55. The good duchess is here.

Part 5 (20 points)
56. Je me demande si elle aime le prince. 57. Je me demande si elle se souvient de moi. 58. Si je ne me trompe pas, il est un duc. 59. Malheureusement, ils se trompent. 60. Les rois parlent beaucoup. 61. Les princes mangent beaucoup de glace. 62. Les rois, que font-ils? 63. Les chiens et les chats peuvent danser.
64. Les riches sont partout les mêmes. 65. Les chats, que mangent-ils

French 2, Semester 1

Section 1

You are about to continue the most exciting adventure of your life. Here are some things to keep in mind as you go through the activities in this section.

After completing this section you will be able to:

- Identify objects from a description.
- Expand cultural knowledge
- Comprehend the meaning of a story and use new vocabulary learned.
- Use feminine vs. masculine object pronouns.
- Use natural vs. arbitrary gender.
- Use entirety vs. part: le, l', les, vs. en.
- Use object pronouns and reflexive pronouns.
- Understand a story of considerable length and retell it in your own words.
- Master object pronouns with finite and infinite verbs.
- Build fluency through repetition.
- Understand the story of "The Three Bears" in French.
- Use geography vocabulary.

☐ **Lesson 1-1**

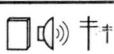

Turn to activity #88 and read and listen to the short description. Concentrate on vocabulary words and how you could use them in your own descriptions. There are culture questions at the end of this activity for you to answer. These culture questions help to reinforce your knowledge about French speaking countries. If you have to look up the answers it's okay. Read the adventure and the culture clips on Morocco. For more information on Morocco visit the web site. You may want to do this in another study session. Remember to gather information for a research paper at the end of the semester.

☐ **1-2**

Who in the "Royal" family speaks Chinese? Open your workbook to activity #89 and find out. This conversation doesn't use pictographs. If you learn

Journal/Notes:

well through pictures you may want to make your own and practice with them. Use your imagination when you are listening to this conversation and try to create your own using a similar format. Work toward fluency in speech and full comprehension in French.

☐ 1-3

Turn to activity #90 and let's do some more grammar. Focus your thinking in French but also try to make connections to your understanding of English grammar. Work both your oral and written skills in this activity. It may take you several study sessions to complete. When you can produce 2-3 of your own French sentences in each focus, move on.

☐ 1-4

Turn to activity #91. You are learning new vocabulary with pictures again. There are various ways to learn this new vocabulary. Choose a method that works best for you and is fun. Do each section of the activity focusing your mind to think and respond in French. This activity may take several study sessions in order to complete each part of the activity. Remember to read the adventure at the end and collect information that will help you solve the mystery.

☐ 1-5

Why do you think the duchess only speaks Chinese at church? Turn to activity #92 and see if you can't find out the answer to this question. This activity will also help you develop your ability to describe an event. Using the examples from the story create your own description of a situation.

☐ 1-6

How well do you know your North American geography? Turn to activity #93 and pretend you are in a French class again studying geography. Use a map to make connections to the knowledge you already have. In French, teach another person the information you learned in this activity.

☐ 1-7

Creative activity. You will need to do a creative project for your portfolio. Take a look at all the recipes on the web site at http://www.powerglide.com/french and make a treat. If at all possible, take an opportunity to have some French speakers participate in this activity with you. Make the recipe, have a French culture day/night and speak French as much as you can. Write about the event and include it in your academic portfolio file. This is just an idea for a creative activity. The possibilities are endless and you may choose one of your own. Remember to create opportunities to use your language skills so it has application to life outside the study session.

☐ 1-8

Children love bedtime stories. Turn to activity #94 and learn a bedtime story in French that you can tell to a child. If you're familiar with this story, cover the English and focus on the French. Make

Journal/Notes:

. . . .

. . . .

. . . .

. . . .

. . . .

notes in English to the side of your French text. Listen to the audio as many times as necessary. Look at the English text and see how close your interpretation is. Draw some pictures that might help you remember vocabulary words and tell the story to some children in French. You may want to set up a story-telling night in conjunction with your local library or other community organization and prepare and tell this story (or the story in Activity 97) in French for your audience. You could count this as one of your portfolio projects. If you do this as a community service project it will look good on scholarship and college applications as well.

☐ **1-9**

Why do children ask so many questions? Have you ever wondered this? Turn to activity #95 and see how many more questions a child can ask a parent. Create some of your own questions from a child's perspective and then answer your own questions with a parent's perspective. If you have a study partner you could answer each other's questions.

☐ **1-10**

Activity #96 is an activity for you to stretch your French comprehension skills. Cover the English text and listen to and read the French text. How much can you understand? Review the French audio until you feel comfortable with the new material. Practice telling the information to another person.

☐ **1-11**

Here's another bedtime story for you to tell in French. Turn to activity #97. Notice how to simplify a story so that all of the information is there, but you can use the target language you know to tell the story. Practice doing this so you can tell an audience.

☐ **1-12**

At the end of activity #97 there are some more culture questions and a culture clip on Senegal. For more information go to the web site and research Senegal. If you want to write your research paper on Senegal, take good notes and record your bibliography information. Remember that you have the entire semester to write your paper so you will want to collect information and keep it together in your academic portfolio file. Continue reading the adventure and making deductions about what will come next.

☐ **1-13**

It's time to review for another test. Testing is just another way to monitor personal progress and understanding. Review vocabulary from conversations and stories, review grammar patterns from the grammar activities, and make sure you can meet all of the objectives of this section. Continue with your study until you are comfortable and then take the online progress test.

Journal/Notes:

. . . .

☐ **1-14**

When you are ready, take the online progress test #7. Go to http://www.power-glide.com/progresstests. Enter your name and e-mail address. Relax, read the instructions carefully and do your best. When you receive the results, review any errors and take the written test.

☐ **1-15**

When you know the results of your progress test, review the areas you struggled with and then take written test #7. If you are pursuing credit, put the results in your academic portfolio folder.

Section 2

I hope you're still excited about your learning adventure. Focus on incorporating the vocabulary and sentences patterns from this section into your everyday conversations in French. Remember that you are capable of learning another language and that learning should be fun and interesting.

After completing this section you will be able to:

- Use geometry vocabulary and identify information described.
- Understand the vocabulary and grammar of stories and lessons and apply those principles to your French conversations.
- Expand your comprehension toward complete understanding.
- Identify objects and ask questions about them.
- Use humor to tell a story.
- Use your imagination to understand and create conversations.
- Articulate the moral of a story.

☐ **Lesson 2-1**

Turn to activity #98. Pretend you're in a French geometry class. Listen to the instructions and then perform the tasks required. Find another person to be your student and teach as much of this lesson as you can in French. If your study partner doesn't speak French, you might want to draw explanations as you teach your information. Don't worry about making a mistake in your speaking; you will continue to build your fluency as you use the language.

☐ **2-2**

Reading is a way to increase vocabulary and build fluency in any language. Turn to activity #99 and listen to and read the information. Concentrate on the new vocabulary and build fluency with it. Cover the English and make notes of what you understand. Review the story as many times as

Journal/Notes:

....
....
....
....
....

needed until you feel comfortable with your comprehension.

☐ 2-3

Turn to activity #100 and see how much geography you can understand in French. You should be able to do this activity well by now, although you will still learn new vocabulary. You should be able to understand the majority of the information from context. Listen to the audio and read through the French until you have the majority of the information and can tell at least 5 facts in French to another person. Continue with the adventure. Are you any closer to solving the mystery?

☐ 2-4

Do you have enough French vocabulary that you could describe an aquarium shark to a group of 7 year-olds? Write down what you might say. Then turn to activity #101 and see if you included some of the same information as in this activity. How much more could you say now? After listening to this activity find someone and describe an aquarium shark to him or her. How interesting can you make your presentation?

☐ 2-5

Turn to activity #102 and listen to the description of the picture given in French. Follow the instructions. If you have a study partner ask and answer each other's questions.

☐ 2-6

Turn to activity #103. Read both the English and the French versions of the story. What is the moral to this story? Can you articulate it? When you rewrite the ending, will it change the moral? Can you articulate that? Work toward being able to tell the story, articulate a moral, and write a new ending and either articulate another moral or at least an opinion.

☐ 2-7

Pretend you are in a French Chemistry class. Turn to activity #104. You will want two glasses of water, one hot, and one cold. You will also want an ice cube, some salt, sugar, sand, and an empty glass. Listen to the French audio two or three times and then go back and perform 2 experiments listening only to the French audio. (Use the pause button as needed.) Choose one of the experiments and teach it to another person using only French. How well can you do it? You may want to perform this for your video portfolio project. In order to understand the new vocabulary and sentence patterns needed to complete this activity in a simulated setting, you may need several study sessions. Take what you need but don't let it become a tedious process, it should be fun.

☐ 2-8

Open your workbook to activities #105 and #106. You will find a short French poem and another humorous short story. Learn them like you have other stories and tell them to someone else.

Journal/Notes:

☐ 2-9

A duchess who speaks Chinese at church and who speaks Russian in the tower. What is next? Turn to activity #107 and find out what is going on with the "Royal" family. Use the patterns you learn here to expand your grammar skills in conversation. Continue your adventure.

☐ 2-10

Take some time to see what La Mouche is up to and how you can help him solve his mystery.

☐ 2-11

It's time for another progress test #8. Prepare for your online test by reviewing each activity to refresh your memory of vocabulary and grammar patterns. When you are ready, go to http://www.power-glide.com/progresstests. Enter your name and e-mail address, relax and take the test.

☐ 2-12

After you review the results of your online progress test, review the material you missed and take written test #8. Correct it and place the corrected test in your academic portfolio folder.

Section 3

You are almost finished with the first semester of second-year French. This section concentrates heavily on reading skills. Reading will improve your language acquisition skills; it will increase your vocabulary, improve your comprehension, and develop speaking patterns that are like a native French speaker. Your ability to create your own thoughts will happen more naturally as well. Use the lesson plan as a guide to use the information you learn in the readings applicable to your everyday speech.

After completing this section you will be able to:

- Rewrite the ending to a story.
- Understand vocabulary and grammar pattern through repetition.
- Expand comprehension, fluency, and use of past and present tense.
- Follow a conversation and understand its meaning.
- Use simple phrases to expand conversations.
- Follow a story line with full comprehension.
- Master new vocabulary.

☐ Lesson 3-1

Turn to activity #108 and read a humorous story. Read both the English and the French versions and then listen to the French version until you know enough vocabulary to rewrite the ending and tell the story to another person. Remember

Journal/Notes:

that when you articulate something to another person you remember it longer.

☐ 3-2

Open your workbook to activity #109 and read the story of "The Farmer and the Turnip." This story is long but uses repetition to help you build fluency. Practice the story until you can tell another person the story. You may want to make pictures to help you tell the story.

☐ 3-3

"The sky is falling!" Who does that sound like? Turn to activity #110 and read about Chicken Little. Cover up the English and focus on the French. Find someone and tell him or her the story. You may even want to perform the story as part of your portfolio presentation if you haven't already done one. If you do practice the story well enough so that the story flows without hesitations.

☐ 3-4

How about a little dry humor? Turn to activity #111. Cover the English and go through the French. Can you understand the punch line? Review it again before you look at the English. Tell this to another person. Take some time to go on another adventure with La Mouche. There are many possibilities for different adventures. Have you chosen the different options?

☐ 3-5

There is always a need to have some catchy phrases in your vocabulary as conversation pieces. Turn to activity #112 and see how many snatches of conversations you can add to your vocabulary base. Make up your own conversations using these pieces of conversations. Can you make a conversation that makes sense?

☐ 3-6

Have you ever wanted to know how to strike up a conversation with someone? Turn to activity #113 see how Vincent strikes up a conversation. Add these phrases to your vocabulary base. Start using them with your friends and family.

☐ 3-7

Activity #114 is similar to the activity you just did. Using these phrases create your own dialogue in French. Use some of these sayings with your family and friends.

☐ 3-8

You are finished with all of the activities for this section. In order to review, look over the vocabulary from the stories and your notes if you've taken them. In addition, review how the grammar works in each activity and see if you can mentally place a rule with it or form another sentence similar to it. Before taking the test make sure you can meet all of the objectives of this section.

Journal/Notes:

☐ 3-9

Are you ready for progress test #9? Go to http://www.power-glide.com/progresstests and fill in your name and e-mail address. Click test #9, relax, and do your best.

☐ 3-10

Look over your test results and review any aspect of the section that you may still have trouble comprehending. When you have sufficiently reviewed take test #9. Have it corrected and include the results in your academic portfolio folder.

> *If you are seeking credit for this course, review the How to Receive Credit information in the Overview at the beginning of this Guide. You will need to have a completed portfolio according to the specifications in the Overview.*

Journal/Notes:

French Test 7

Name_____
Total _____/100 points

PART 1
(15 points) Match the English phrase with the French translation.

1. ____ to suppose
2. ____ to understand
3. ____ to want
4. ____ he wants
5. ____ to have fear or to be afraid
6. ____ he has fear or he is afraid
7. ____ to know (someone)
8. ____ to know (something)
9. ____ great
10. ____ he and they
11. ____ can, be able
12. ____ he can
13. ____ perhaps
14. ____ the duke alone
15. ____ a little

a. *pouvoir*
b. *formidable*
c. *lui et eux*
d. *il peut*
e. *comprendre*
f. *peut-être*
g. *supposer*
h. *seul le duc*
i. *vouloir*
j. *savoir*
k. *un peu*
l. *il veut*
m. *il a peur*
n. *connaître*
o. *avoir peur*

PART 2
(20 points) Translate from English into French.

16.	a.	The king doesn't like the duchess.	
	b.	He detests her.	
17.	a.	The queen does not like the duke.	
	b.	She detests him.	
18.	a.	He loves her.	
	b.	She loves him.	
19.	a.	The king sees the tower.	
	b.	He sees it.	
20.	a.	The king sees the drum.	
	b.	He sees it.	

21.	a.	He sees the tower and the drum.	
	b.	He sees them.	
22.	a.	The king knows the duke sings.	
	b.	The queen knows it too.	
23.	a.	The king is making the drum.	
	b.	Yes, he is making it.	
24.	a.	He is making the drums.	
	b.	Yes, he is making them.	
25.	a.	He drinks the milk.	
	b.	He drinks it.	

PART 3
(15 points) Translate from French into English.

26.	*Il me voit.*	
27.	*Je me vois.*	
28.	*Il le voit.*	
29.	*Il se voit.*	
30.	*Elle se voit.*	
31.	*Ils les voient.*	
32.	*Ils se voient.*	
33.	*Elle se demande.*	
34.	*Je me demande.*	
35.	*Je me trompe.*	
36.	*Il se trompe.*	
37.	*Je me prépare.*	
38.	*Il va se préparer.*	

| 39. | *Elle dit qu'elle va se préparer.* | |
| 40. | *Elle décide de se préparer.* | |

PART 4

(20 points—2 points each) Read the story in French and then answer the French questions below in English.

Il y a trois océans principaux sur notre planète: l'Atlantique, le Pacifique, et l'océan Indien. Les Etats-Unis d'Amérique sont situés dans l'hémisphère Nord, sur le continent Nord Américain. Les USA ont une frontière avec le Canada au Nord et le Méxique au Sud. Les Etats-Unis d'Amérique sont composés de cinquante Etats; quarante-huit sont sur le continent, un est tout là-haut au Nord, et l'autre est là-bas au milieu de l'Océan Pacifique. L'Alaska est l'état le plus étendu, le Texas est le second et la Californie est le troisième. La Californie est un célèbre Etat situé sur la côte Ouest, la côte Pacifique. Los Angeles et San Francisco sont deux villes célèbres de Californie. La capitale des Etats-Unis n'est pas New-York mais Washington D.C. (District de Colombie.) Washington est une ville sur la côte Est, la côte Atlantique.

41. *Combien d'Etats composent les USA?*

42. *Quelle est la capitale des USA?*

43. *Quels sont les deux villes célèbres de Californie?*

44. *Deux pays font frontière avec les Etats-Unis, les quels?*

45. *Nommez les trois océans principaux.*

46. *Quel est l'Etat le plus étendu?*

47. *Washington D.C. se trouve sur quelle côte?*

PART 5

(20 points—2 points each) Fill in the translations in French and English.

48.	Mama, why do we have two cars?	
49.		*Parce que Papa et moi en avons besoin chacun d'une.*
50.	Why does Daddy need a car?	
51.		*Parce qu'il doit conduire pour aller au travail.*
52.	Why do you need a car?	

53.		*Parce que je dois aller faire les commissions.*
54.	Why don't I have a car too?	
55.		*Pourquoi aurais-tu besoin d'une voiture?*
56.	To drive to the moon.	
57.		*Oh, ne sois pas bête!*

PART 6—LISTENING COMPREHENSION

(10 points) Read the statements below. Then listen to the Chatter at a Royal Ball on the comprehension audio and determine if the statements are T (True) or F (False) based on what you've heard. The story will be repeated twice on the audio.

58. _____ According to the text, the duke speaks five languages.

59. _____ It is possible that the duke speaks Chinese.

60. _____ He likes to speak it as often as he can.

61. _____ The princess speaks Chinese very well.

62. _____ She doesn't speak it very often.

63. _____ She speaks Chinese in church.

64. _____ She likes to speak it in the palace.

65. _____ The king doesn't like Chinese spoken in the palace.

66. _____ She attends church with a lot of Chinese people.

67. _____ She also speaks Chinese with the king.

French Test 8

Name _____
Total _____ /100 points

PART 1

(20 points—2 points each) Translate from French into English.

1.	*Regarde ce grand poisson.*	
2.	*C'est un requin.*	
3.	*Les requins vivent dans les océans.*	
4.	*Ils ont beaucoup de dents bien aiguisées.*	
5.	*Leur peau n'est pas lisse comme la tienne.*	
6.	*Elle est très rugueuse, comme du papier de verre.*	
7.	*Les requins sont dangereux.*	
8.	*Ils sont méchants.*	
9.	*Ils n'ont aucune peur.*	
10.	*Certains requins attaquent les gens.*	

PART 2

(20 points—2 points each) Match the English words and phrases with the French translations.

11. _____ to learn
12. _____ to hear
13. _____ to meet, encounter
14. _____ to fall from/off a tower
15. _____ to respond
16. _____ crazy things
17. _____ so many languages
18. _____ to fall in love
19. _____ about which
20. _____ way out here

a. *tomber d'une tour*
b. *tomber amoureux/amoureuse*
c. *répondre*
d. *apprendre*
e. *dont*
f. *des bêtises*
g. *entendre*
h. *tant de langues*
i. *tout là-bas*
j. *rencontrer*

PART 3

(20 points—2 points each) Respond in English to the following questions after reading the French story below.

Un fils paresseux

Un fils se plaignait à son père: "Je ne veux pas aller à l'école." Le père dit: "Jeannot, donne-moi trois raisons de ne pas y aller." Le fils répondit: "Je m'ennuie à l'école. Il faut travailler trop dur, et mes professeurs ne m'aiment pas." "Je comprends tes sentiments, Jeannot. Parfois, j'ai ressenti la même chose. Laisse-moi te donner trois raisons d'y aller: Nous devons faire certaines choses, même si nous n'en avons pas envie. Tu as 47 ans. Tu es le principal!"

List the three reasons why the father thinks it is important for the son to go to school:

21.
22.
23.

24. Translate the French expression "*se plaignait*" into English._____

List the three reasons why the son does not want to attend school.

25.
26.
27.

28. Translate the title of the story into English.

29. True or False: Johnny's father does not understand his son's feelings.

30. True or False: Johnny wanted to go to school that day.

PART 4

(20 points—2 points each) Translate from French into English.

31.	*Un petit garçon trouva une jolie fleur.*	
32.	*Alors il cueillit la fleur.*	
33.	*La soeur prit la fleur.*	
34.	*La soeur apporta la fleur à son père.*	
35.	*Voici, prends-la!*	
36.	*Merci, cher mari.*	
37.	*Cette fleur est pour toi, de moi.*	

38.	*Elle dit je t'aime.*	
39.	*Le père prit la fleur.*	
40.	*J'aime ma soeur.*	

PART 5—DICTATION

(20 points—1 point each line and 5 points extra credit) You will hear a telephone conversation between a young child and an adult three different times. Use the vocabulary provided below to write what you hear. You'll want to pause the audio frequently as you do this dictation exercise.

a	*a-t-il*	*allô*	*avec*	*bien*	*d'autre*	*d'eux*
dis-moi	*eh*	*elle*	*est*	*est-ce*	*est-il*	*et*
font	*ils*	*l'un*	*là*	*lui*	*maman*	*n'y*
occupés	*oh*	*parler*	*pas*	*père*	*personne*	*pourquoi*
problème	*puis-je*	*qu'est-ce*	*qu'il*	*qu'ils*	*que*	*qui*
sont	*ta*	*un*	*y*	*ton*		

41. (Whisper): _____ .

42. (Caller): _____ , _____ _____ _____ _____ _____ ___ ?

    (Whisper): *Ouiii.*

43. (Caller): _____ _____ _____ _____ ?

    (Whisper): *Nnnon.*

44. (Caller): ____ _____ _____ ?

    (Whisper): *Elle est occupée.*

45. (Caller): _____ _____ , _____ ____ ?

    (Whisper): *Ouiii.*

46. (Caller): _____ _____ _____ _____ ?

    (Whisper): *Nnnon.*

47. (Caller): ____ _____ _____ ?

    (Whisper): *Il est occupé.*

48. (Caller): ____ _____ , _____ _____ ___ __ _____ _____ _____ ___ ?

    (Whisper): *Ouiii.*

49. (Caller): _____ ?

85

(Whisper): *Mmm.*

50. (Caller): _____? _____.

    (Whisper): *Des voisins et des policiers*

51. (Caller): ____, __ _____ ___ _____?

    (Whisper): *Nnnon.*

52. (Caller): _____ _____ _____ _____ _____?

    (Whisper): *Nnnon.*

53. (Caller): ____ _____ _____?

54. (Whisper): _____ _____ _____.

55. (Caller): ____ _____, _____ _____ _____?

    (Whisper): *Ils me cherchent.*

French Test 9

Name _____
Total _____/100 points

PART 1
(40 points—2 points each) Translate the French phrases into English.

1.	*Je suis américain.*	
2.	*Je suis aussi une fleuriste américaine.*	
3.	*Très intéressant!*	
4.	*Je m'appelle Sophie.*	
5.	*C'est un plaisir.*	
6.	*Pour moi aussi.*	
7.	*Qui est-ce?*	
8.	*C'est moi.*	
9.	*Votre nom, monsieur?*	
10.	*Nous sommes avec vous.*	
11.	*Ne vous inquiétez pas.*	
12.	*OK, venez avec moi.*	
13.	*Allons-y!*	
14.	*Attendez.*	
15.	*Vite!*	
16.	*Parlez-vous espagnol ou allemand?*	
17.	*Non, mais je parle un petit peu italien.*	
18.	*Bien sûr.*	
19.	*Combien voulez-vous de moi?*	

| 20. | *Combien ça coûte?* | |

PART 2
(20 points—2 points each) Translate the English phrases into French.

21.	Louder!	
22.	I agree.	
23.	They're thieves.	
24.	What's that?	
25.	Waiter!	
26.	I hear you.	
27.	I've been studying English for years.	
28.	Right away.	
29.	Allow me to introduce myself.	
30.	It's a pleasure to meet you.	

PART 3
(20 points—2 points each) Read the following exchange in French. Then answer the questions below.

Personne ne s'intéresse à moi!

Docteur: *Veuillez entrer. Asseyez-vous!*
Patient: *Merci, docteur.*
Docteur: *Dites-moi, quel est votre problème?*
Patient: *Oh, docteur, s'il vous plaît, aidez-moi.*
              Dites-moi ce que je dois faire.
              J'ai l'impression de n'avoir aucune valeur.
              J'ai l'impression que personne ne s'intéresse à moi.
              Personne ne fait attention à moi.
              Tout le monde me traite comme si je ne comptais pas.
              Tout le monde me traite comme si je n'existais même pas.
Docteur: *Au suivant!*

31.   True or False: The doctor solves the patient's problem.

32.   Translate the French sentence "*Veuillez entrer*" into English.

33.	List five reasons why the patient is unhappy.

33.

34.

35.

36.

37.

38.	True or False: The patient has a physical illness.

39.	Translate the title from French to English.

40.	True or False: The doctor tells the patient to lie down.

PART 4—DICTATION

(20 points—1 point each line) You will hear a reduced version of "The Three Little Pigs" three different times. Use the vocabulary provided below to write what you hear. You'll want to pause the audio frequently as you do this dictation exercise.

à	*affamé*	*briques*	*cochon*	*cochons*	*de*	*en*
est	*et*	*fois*	*frères*	*il*	*la*	*le*
loup	*mais*	*maison*	*maisons*	*ne*	*paille*	*part*
pas	*petit*	*petits*	*planches*	*plus*	*s'échappe*	*souffle*
tombe	*très*	*trois*	*un*	*une*	*Arrive*	*Revient*

41. _____ _____ _____ . _____ . _____ _____ .

42. _____ _____ ___ _____ .

43. _____ _____ ___ _____ .

44. _____ _____ ___ _____ .

45. ___ _____ . ___ _____ _____ .

46. ___ _____ __ ___ _____ ___ _____ .

47. ___ _____ .

48. ___ _____ ___ _____ _____ .

49. _____ ___ _____ _____ _____ .

50. ___ _____ _____ _____ ___ _____ .

89

51. ___ _____ __ _____ ___ _____.
52. ___ _____ _____ _____. ___ _____.
53. ___ _____ ___ _____ ___ _____.
54. ___ ___ _____ _____ _____.
55. _____ _____ ___ _____ ___ _____.
56. ____ _____ __ _____ _____.
57. ____ _____ _____. ___ _____.
58. ____ _____ ____ _____ _____.
59. _____ ___ _____ _____ ___ _____ _____.
60. ____ ___ _____ _____ _____ _____.

French Test 7 Answers

PART 1 (15 POINTS)
1. g. 2. e. 3. i. 4. l. 5. o. 6. m. 7. n. 8. j.
9. b. 10. c. 11. a. 12. d. 13. f. 14. h. 15. k.

PART 2 (20 POINTS)
16. *a. Le roi n'aime pas la duchesse. b. Il la déteste.*
17. *a. La reine n'aime pas le duc. b. Elle le déteste.*
18. *a. Il l'aime. b. Elle l'aime.* 19. *a. Le roi voit la tour. b. Il la voit.* 20. *a. Le roi voit le tambour. b. Il le voit.* 21. *a. Il voit la tour et le tambour. b. Il les voit.* 22. *a. Le roi sait que le duc chante. b. La reine le sait aussi.* 23. *a. Le roi fait le tambour. b. Oui, il le fait.* 24. *a. Il fait les tambours. b. Oui, il les fait.*
25. *a. Il boit le lait. b. Il le boit.*

PART 3 (15 POINTS)
26. He sees me. 27. I see myself. 28. He sees him (it). 29. He sees himself. 30. She sees herself.
31. They see them. 32. They see themselves. 33. She wonders (asks herself). 34. I wonder (ask myself).
35. I am mistaken. 36. He is mistaken. 37. I am preparing myself. 38. He is going to prepare himself.
39. She says she's going to prepare herself. 40. She decides to prepare herself.

PART 4 (20 POINTS)
41. 50 States 42. Washington D.C. 43. a. Los Angeles b. San Francisco 44. Mexico and Canada
45. a. Indian b. Pacific c. Atlantic 46. Alaska
47. East Coast

PART 5 (20 POINTS)
48. *Maman, pourquoi avons-nous deux voitures?*
49. Because Daddy and I need one each. 50. *Pourquoi est-ce que Papa a besoin d'une voiture?* 51. Because he has to drive to work. 52. *Pourquoi est-ce que toi, tu as besoin d'une voiture?* 53. Because I have to do the shopping. 54. *Et moi, pourquoi je n'ai pas aussi une voiture?* 55. What would you need a car for? 56. *Pour conduire jusqu'à la lune.* 57. Oh, don't be silly!

PART 6 (10 POINTS)
58. F 59. T 60. F 61. T 62. T 63. T 64. F
65. T 66. T 67. F

French Test 8 Answers

PART 1 (20 POINTS)
1. Look at that big fish. 2. It's a shark. 3. Sharks live in oceans. 4. They have a lot of sharp teeth. 5. Their skin is not smooth like yours. 6. It's very rough, like sandpaper. 7. Sharks are dangerous. 8. They're mean.
9. They're fearless. 10. Some sharks attack people.

PART 2 (20 POINTS)
11. d 12. g 13. j 14. a 15. c 16. f 17. h 18. b
19. e 20. i

PART 3 (20 POINTS)
21. There are things we should do even if we don't like them. 22. You are 47 years old. 23. You are the principal. 24. complained 25. I am bored at school.
26. There's too much work to do. 26. My teachers don't like me. 28. A lazy son 29. F 30. F

PART 4 (20 POINTS)
31. A little boy found a pretty flower. 32. So he picked the flower. 33. The sister took the flower. 34. The sister took the flower to her father. 35. Here, take this!
36. Thank you, dear husband. 37. This flower is for you from me. 38. It (the flower) says that I love you.
39. The father took the flower. 40. I love my sister.

PART 5 (20 POINTS)
41. *Allô.* 42. *Allô, est-ce que ta maman est là?*
43. *Puis-je parler avec elle?* 44. *Et pourquoi pas?*
45. *Ton père, est-il là?* 46. *Puis-je parler avec lui?*
47. *Et pourquoi pas?* 48. *Eh bien, est-ce qu'il n'y a pas d'autres personnes là?* 49. *Qui?* 50. *Qui? Dis-moi.* 51. *Oh, y a-t-il un problème?* 52. *Puis-je parler avec l'un d'eux?* 53. *Et pourquoi pas?* 54. *Ils sont occupés.* 55. *Eh bien, qu'est-ce qu'ils font?*

French Test 9 Answers

PART 1 (40 POINTS)
1. I am American. 2. I am also an American florist.
3. Very interesting! 4. My name is Sophie. 5. It's a pleasure. 6. Same here. 7. Who's there? 8. It's me.
9. Your name, mister? 10. We are with you.
11. Don't worry. 12. OK, come with me. 13. Let's go! 14. Wait. 15. Hurry! 16. Do you speak Spanish

or German? 17. No, but I speak Italian a little bit.
18. Of course. 19. How much do you want from me?
20. How much does this cost?

PART 2 (20 POINTS)
21. *Plus fort!* 22. *Je suis d'accord.* 23. *Ce sont des voleurs.* 24. *Qu'est-ce que c'est?* 25. *Garçon!* 26. *Je vous écoute.* 27. *J'étudie l'anglais depuis des années.* 28. *Tout de suite.* 29. *Permettez-moi de me présenter.* 30. *Enchanté de faire votre connaissance.*

PART 3 (20 POINTS)
31. F 32. Please come in. 33. I feel I am worthless.
34. I feel no one cares about me. 35. No one pays attention to me. 36. Everyone treats me as if I didn't matter. 37. Everyone treats me as if I didn't even exist.
38. F 39. No one pays attention to me! 40. F

PART 4 (20 POINTS)
41. Trois petits cochons. Frères. Trois maisons.
42. Une maison en paille. 43. Une maison en planches.
44. Une maison en briques. 45. Un loup. Il vient affamé. 46. Il vient à la maison en paille. 47. Il souffle. 48. La maison en paille tombe. 49. Mais le petit cochon s'échappe. 50. Le loup vient une fois de plus. 51. Il vient à la maison en planches. 52. Il vietn très affamé. Il souffle. 53. La maison en planches tombe. 54. Mais le petit cochon s'échappe. 55. Le loup vient une fois de plus. 56. Il vient à la maison en briques. 57. Il est très affamé. Il souffle. 58. Il souffle une fois de plus. 59. Mais la maison en briques ne tombe pas. 60. Et le loup part très très affamé.

French Test 7 Transcript

- ••: Only the duke speaks Chinese, right?
- •: No. He doesn't speak it. Perhaps he understands it a little.
- ••: I suppose he <u>can</u> speak it, but he doesn't <u>want</u> to speak it.
- •: Oh, that's possible.
- ••: It's the princess that speaks it well.
- •: But she doesn't speak it often; she speaks it only at church.
- ••: I believe she likes to speak it there, but she doesn't like to speak it in the palace.
- •: With good reason. The king detests it.
- ••: And with whom does she speak Chinese at the church?
- •: Oh, she knows many Chinese who go to church with her.
- ••: And she talks it with them?
- •: I believe so.
- ••: Great!

Seul le duc parle chinois, n'est-ce pas?
Non. Il ne le parle pas. Peut-être il le comprend un peu.
Je suppose qu'il <u>peut</u> le parler, mais il ne <u>veut</u> pas le parler.
Oh, c'est possible.
C'est la princesse qui le parle bien.
Mais elle ne le parle pas souvent; elle ne le parle qu'à l'église.
Je crois qu'elle aime le parler à l'église, mais elle n'aime pas le parler dans le palais.
Elle a de bonnes raisons. Le roi le déteste.
Et avec qui parle-t-elle chinois à l'église?
Oh, elle connaît beaucoup de Chinois qui vont à l'église avec elle.
Et elle le parle avec eux?
Je crois que oui.
Formidable!

French Test 8 Transcript

IS YOUR MOTHER THERE?
Est-ce que ta maman est là?

A small child's voice answers the telephone in a muffled whisper, as if in a closet.

(Whisper):	Hellooo.	*Allô.*
(Caller):	Hello. Is your mother there?	*Allô, est-ce que ta maman est là?*
(Whisper):	Yeees.	*Ouiii.*
(Caller):	May I talk with her?	*Puis-je parler avec elle?*
(Whisper):	Nooo.	*Nnnon.*
(Caller):	Why not?	*Et pourquoi pas?*
(Whisper):	She's buzzzyy.	*Elle est occupée.*
(Caller):	Is your father there?	*Ton père, est-il là?*
(Whisper):	Yeees.	*Ouiii.*
(Caller):	May I talk with him?	*Puis-je parler avec lui?*
(Whisper):	Nooo.	*Nnnon.*
(Caller):	Why not?	*Et pourquoi pas?*
(Whisper):	She's buzzzyy.	*Il est occupé.*
(Caller):	Well, is anyone else there?	*Eh bien, est-ce qu'il n'y a pas d'autres personnes là?*
(Whisper):	Yeees.	*Ouiii.*
(Caller):	Who?	*Qui?*
(Whisper):	Mmm.	*Mmm.*

(Caller):	Who? Tell me.	*Qui? Dis-moi.*
(Whisper):	Some neighbors and some police.	*Des voisins et des policiers*
(Caller):	Oh, is there something wrong?	*Oh, y a-t-il un problème?*
(Whisper):	Nooo.	*Nnnon.*
(Caller):	Well could I talk with one of them?	*Puis-je parler avec l'un d'eux?*
(Whisper):	Nooo.	*Nnnon.*
(Caller):	Why not?	*Et pourquoi pas?*
(Whisper):	They're all buzzzyy.	*Ils sont occupés.*
(Caller):	Well what are they doing?	*Eh bien, qu'est-ce qu'ils font?*
(Whisper):	They're looking for me.	*Ils me cherchent.*

French Test 9 Transcript

THE THREE LITTLE PIGS
Les trois petits cochons

41	*Trois petits cochons. Frères. Trois maisons.*	Three little pigs. Brothers. Three houses.
42	*Une maison en paille.*	A house of straw.
43	*Une maison en planches.*	A house of sticks.
44	*Une maison en briques.*	A house of bricks.
45	*Un loup. Il vient affamé.*	A wolf. He comes hungry.
46	*Il vient à la maison en paille.*	He comes to a house of straw.
47	*Il souffle.*	He blows.
48	*La maison en paille tombe.*	The house of straw falls.
49	*Mais le petit cochon s'échappe.*	But the little pig escapes.
50	*Le loup vient une fois de plus.*	The wolf comes once again.
51	*Il vient à la maison en planches.*	He comes to a house of sticks.
52	*Il vient très affamé. Il souffle.*	He comes very hungry. He blows.
53	*La maison en planches tombe.*	The house of sticks falls.
54	*Mais le petit cochon s'échappe.*	But the little pig escapes.
55	*Le loup vient une fois de plus.*	The wolf comes once again.
56	*Il vient à la maison en briques.*	He comes to a house of bricks.
57	*Il est TRES affamé. Il souffle.*	He is VERY hungry. He blows.
58	*Il souffle une fois de plus.*	He blows once again.
59	*Mais la maison en briques ne tombe pas.*	But the house of bricks doesn't fall.
60	*Et le loup part TRES TRES affamé.*	And the wolf leaves VERY VERY hungry.

French 2, Semester 2

Welcome to French 2 Semester 2. French 2 semester 2 focuses on building fluency through reading. You will be exposed to large amounts of information and must decipher what you can personally use to build depth in your conversations and other communication skills. This will happen naturally and may be different for every learner even though the material you are exposed to is the same. Enjoy the learning process.

Section 1

The activities in this section may appear shorter than they are outlined to do in one study session. However, you're concentrating on building your comprehension and fluency so use as many study sessions as needed to complete each activity.

After completing this section you will be able to:
- Increase reading and listening comprehension, and vocabulary usage.
- Read a dialogue for comprehension and then repeat it.
- Recognize your ability to understand French.
- Understand and use geometry vocabulary.
- Expand cultural knowledge.
- Increase the number of useful phrases you can say.

☐ Lesson 1-1

Open your workbook to activity to #115. Here are some more phrases that you can incorporate into your conversations. Focus on the French and use the English as a guide to your understanding. The last section doesn't have an English translation so focus on the meaning and not necessarily exact translations. If you want to translate everything word for word you can but it isn't necessary. Use your 10 new memorized words in conversations of your own.

Journal/Notes:

- -

- -

- -

- -

- -

☐ **1-2**

Turn to activity #116 and learn some more useful phrases and sentences. Again focus on the French more than the English.

☐ **1-3**

In this study session go to the CD-ROM and take another adventure with La Mouche. You should be able to understand most of what is going on in French. If you can't determine what is going on from the context of the conversation, pause the audio, and take some notes. You are really going to have to be a language sleuth. Enjoy learning through this interactive method.

☐ **1-4**

How many people in the "Royal" family can sing? Turn to activity #117 and pay attention to who is doing what! Pretend you are a news commentator or a newspaper columnist and you have to report on what the "Royal" family is doing. What will you say? What will you write? Remember to report the truth! When you're finished with your column go to the next activity.

☐ **1-5**

Activity #118 is a story with a fun message. What is the message? Can you articulate it? Listen to and read the French enough times to incorporate the new vocabulary into your personal conversations. Tell several different audiences the story. Another thing that will help you is to read the French aloud without the audio. This will help you read so you don't sound monotone.

☐ **1-6**

Do you like fables? Fables are stories that teach you a principle. Read activity #119 in French focusing on comprehension and meaning in French. When you know the French version of the story well enough, focus on articulating the principle you learned. How does that relate to your life and the lives of those you live and associate with? It is somewhat more difficult to articulate the meaning of the story with your own opinion and interpretation of the meaning. This will stretch your communication skills to another level. Work toward communication and don't hold back because you may not be able to communicate in perfect grammatical speech.

☐ **1-7**

Have you ever heard of the five blind men who are trying to describe an elephant? Turn to activity #120 and read the story in both English and French. Can you articulate the moral of the story in French? Try to see if you can. Remember to recognize how listening and reading are helping you to gain necessary skills in language learning. Create opportunities to use your language even if it's just to tell a piece of a story. As you continue your study work on telling the entire story without it being memorized.

Journal/Notes:

. . . .

. . . .

. . . .

. . . .

. . . .

☐ **1-8**

Pretend you are an American spy preparing to work in the French-speaking Ivory Coast. Go to the web site http://www.power-glide.com/french/links to find out additional information about the country you are about to enter. What other things might you need to know in order to be better prepared?

☐ **1-9**

This might be a good time to write your own adventure or story for a portfolio project. You have plenty of examples in the activities you've done so far to aid you in this story. You are welcome to write any kind of paper for the writing requirement but you probably have the tools to write your own adventure. Review the adventures with "La Mouche" and use information from the stories you've just learned as keys to unlock your mysteries. What ever you do, be thorough and give yourself plenty of time to write a rough draft, go over it, and produce a final draft.

☐ **1-10**

Review for your progress test by going over vocabulary and grammar patterns in the stories. When you feel you know the information well, take the online progress test.

☐ **1-11**

Go to http://www.power-glide.com/progresstests and take progress test #10. Fill in the information requested and relax and enjoy showing off your language skills. When your receive your score, review and correct any errors and prepare for your written test.

☐ **1-12**

Take written test #10. Have it corrected and put the results in your academic portfolio file.

Section 2

Do you realize that you when you complete this section you'll be almost finished with this course? What can you learn in this section that will help you speak French more effectively? This is another short section but you need to focus on building fluency and using new vocabulary and grammar in your own personal French conversations.

After completing this section you will be able to:

- Listen to a French story and maintain comprehension without the help of an English text.
- Pick out important phrases from stories and use them in your own conversations.

Journal/Notes:

- -

- -

- -

- -

- -

- Read stories in French and recognize comprehension and understand new vocabulary from context.
- Read to increase all skill levels of language learning.

☐ Lesson 2-1

Open your workbook to activity #121. This activity doesn't have an English text to look at while you listen to the audio. Have confidence in yourself and your abilities to understand French. Notice how the story has been simplified so that you can understand it and also retell it. Take notes to help you understand.

☐ 2-2

Turn to activity #122 and read another version of the "Three Little Pigs." You will notice right off that this version is much more in depth than the one you completed in your last study session. Learning this version may take you several study sessions. Remember to listen to the entire story and then go back and work paragraph sections until you can tell the main idea of each paragraph. Then begin to put paragraphs together in your own words focusing on the flow of your storytelling. You may want to draw pictures as visual clues. You may want to do another community storytelling night at a school or library. Practice the story until you can retell it with inflection and enthusiasm.

☐ 2-3

Turn to activity #123 and read another story. Remember to recognize how listening and reading are helping you to gain necessary skills in language learning. Retell the story using words and phrases from the story. By doing this, you will increase your ability to produce more language skills.

☐ 2-4

Turn to activity #124 and read a very short story. Focus on the French so you can rewrite the ending. Can you tell the story to another person as well as articulate your opinion? Work toward expressing your own ideas about what you read.

☐ 2-5

At the end of activity #124 there are culture questions to answer and more culture research to do. Spend some time researching Switzerland. You may want to use Switzerland in your research paper or you may want to write your own adventure story using the Swiss culture as your theme. Whatever creative project you decide to do, make sure you do a thorough job.

☐ 2-6

Turn to activity #125 and listen to a French only version of "The Silent Fisherman." What new conclusions can you come up with? How many more words can you understand and use in your

Journal/Notes:

own conversations? Are you making opportunities to use your French?

☐ 2-7 🔊

Activity #126 is another famous story with a message. Work on building your fluency and articulating the message of the story to another person. Just telling the story is one thing but adding your opinion or teaching the message of the story involves some additional thought and practice with your new language. Take the time to sort out your thoughts and put them into French.

☐ 2-8 🔊

Turn to activity #127 in your workbook. As you listen and read the story your main focus is to build your vocabulary. The next step is to do something with the new vocabulary you're learning. Telling the story to another person is a good way to use what you just learned. What are some other ways you can use your new material to solidify your vocabulary retention?

☐ 2-9

Turn to activity #128. Here are some proverbial sayings that will make you sound like you know a lot of French. Try to think of situations where you could use these phrases. Try to use at least three after the first study session.

☐ 2-10 🔊

How does repetition help you learn? Turn to activity #129 and read the story of "The Little Red Hen." Use the repetition of the story to build fluency in retelling the story. Retell this story to at least 2 different people.

☐ 2-11 🔊

As you read you will discover that each story has its own flavor. Turn to activity #130. As you read and listen to this story, what flavor does it have? Do you like this flavor or do prefer a different one? Does the story have a different flavor in French than it does in English? Tell the story to another person. What do they think?

☐ 2-12

Activity #131 is a very different type of activity. By now you understand that Power-Glide activities don't supply you with a list of vocabulary to study and then isolate that vocabulary with a few grammar patterns. In direct opposite to that, we give you so much vocabulary that you have to learn to take what you can use and make it apply to your personal conversations and situations. Here is an activity that will help show you how much you know in a categorized form. In addition to the instructions try to create a conversation or a story incorporating the vocabulary you haven't picked up on to this point. Share your conversation or story with your study partner or a family member. You may want to make flashcards or a game of concentration to help you study these words.

Journal/Notes:

☐ 2-13

Prepare to take online progress test #11 by reviewing vocabulary and grammar as outlined in each activity. Prepare well and take the test when you are ready. Can you meet the objectives of this section? When you can take the online progress test by going to http://www.power-glide.com/progresstests. You know the routine by now so relax and good luck.

☐ 2-14

When you review your progress test and study anything you missed, take written test #11. Have your test graded and include the results in your academic portfolio folder.

Section 3

This is the last section in your French course. Can you believe it? In this last section you will continue to build vocabulary and fluency through reading. Take the time to use the vocabulary you learn in other settings and in your French conversations with others.

After completing this section you will be able to:

- Build comprehension and vocabulary through reading.
- Read and comprehend stories that are longer.
- Expand cultural knowledge.

☐ Lesson 3-1

Turn to activity #132 in your workbook. This is another reading of Little Red Riding Hood. Cover up the English and listen to the story in French. Make notes of vocabulary and grammar that might be new to you or that you don't remember. Review those words or phrases that are new, or that you didn't remember until you feel comfortable with them and can use them in sentences of your own. Try to retell the story with more complexity this time around. Remember each time you listen to and retell a story your ability to use more vocabulary increases. Think of ways you can use this information in other settings.

☐ 3-2

La fantaisie d'une laitiere. Turn to activity #133 and read this French story. What is the moral to the story? Can you articulate it? How many new words and phrases can you come up with? Can you write your own fantasy? Use the material you learn in this activity to build your own conversations in French.

Journal/Notes:

☐ 3-3

Activity #134 is another short story with a moral. Read through the English and the French and then work toward fluency in reading and speaking French. Use the story to teach your family members the lesson that lies within. You will need to practice articulating your own message so rehearse your lesson before you make your presentation.

☐ 3-4

Activity #135 is another version of "The Little Red Hen." This version is more complicated and uses additional grammar and vocabulary to facilitate more intrigue when telling the story. Practice using these more complex sentences, changing vocabulary as you need to build your language skills. Prepare and tell this story with intrigue to at least 2 audiences.

☐ 3-5

Activity #136 is a story that uses repetition to teach. You will learn some additional animal words through this story. Draw pictures of each animal and tell the story to your family. Use the pictures of the animals and describe them in a different context. You may even want to create your own story. If you do, you can submit it as part of your portfolio. Have fun learning and keep in mind that stories can teach you more things than just vocabulary.

☐ 3-6

Activity #137 is a story of considerable length. Listen to the story with the audio and covering the English. Make notes as you go along. It doesn't matter how long it takes you to get through the story. Focus on full comprehension in French. Read the French story aloud without the audio as well to help your reading fluency. Read the story again silently to yourself. Is there a difference in your listening comprehension and your reading comprehension? Read the English version. Did you understand the entire story? As you continue to read in French, you will find that your ability to comprehend will also increase. Keep moving forward.

☐ 3-7

Activity #138 is another short story with a moral. Do the same thing as you have done before in preparing to teach this story to another person. What is the message? Can you articulate it? Can you ask questions about the story so you audience figures the message out on their own?

☐ 3-8

Are you ready for one last story? Turn to activity #139. This story doesn't have audio so read it on your own. Try to read it both orally and silently. Try to figure out the meaning of new words from context and if you are still stumped, look at the English translation. What do you think about this story? If you had to teach the point of the story what would you say? How can you use what you

Journal/Notes:

learned from the story and apply it to other areas of your language learning?

☐ 3-9 ☐ ††

At the end of activity #139 the adventure continues with a look at Tahitian culture. Read the culture clip and then venture to the web site to search for more information on Tahiti. Have you already written your research paper on a country and its culture? This may be a good time to begin the research if you haven't done it. If you've completed your research paper this might be a good time to do another one of your portfolio projects. Don't forget to continue the adventure in your workbook so you know the ending.

☐ 3-10 ☐

On page 324 of your workbook there is a culture test. Take it and see how much you can remember. What you don't remember you can look up on your notes.

☐ 3-11 ☐

Creative Project: Page 325 in your workbook has a recipe for French Crepes. Get a group of people together and make crepes. You can choose another recipe from the web site if you don't like this one. Make an event of it. If you have a French cuisine store near you, go and purchase ingredients for a recipe using your French. Write about your experience. (This is only an example of the possibilities, come up with an idea that you can do in your area.)

Journal/Notes:

- -
- -
- -
- -
- -

☐ 3-12

If you haven't finished your adventures with La Mouche, continue to take adventures even though you are finished with your workbook. Doing the interactive adventures periodically with help you stay on top of your language. Also make opportunities to use the language daily.

☐ 3-13 💡

Prepare for the online progress test #12 by reviewing the vocabulary and information in this last section. When you are ready, take the online progress test by going to http://www.power-glide.com/progresstests.

☐ 3-14 ✓

When you have the results of your progress tests, and have reviewed your errors, take test #12. Have the test corrected and add it to your academic portfolio.

> *If you are seeking credit for this course, review the How to Receive Credit information in the Overview at the beginning of this Guide. You will need to have a completed portfolio according to the specifications in the Overview.*

French Test 10

Name _____
Total _____/100 points

PART 1
(14 points—2 points each) Translate the English phrases into French.

1.	I understand that.	
2.	But now my father is angry with me.	
3.	Such is life.	
4.	Are you (*tu* form) looking for a job?	
5.	Where do you (*tu* form) work now?	
6.	At the bookstore.	
7.	What is her name?	

PART 2
(20 points—2 points each) Translate the French phrases into English.

8.	*Qui chante?*	
9.	*Le roi. Le roi chante.*	
10.	*Quel roi?*	
11.	*Bobi et Misti chantent aussi.*	
12.	*Le roi qui aime jouer du tambour chante maintenant, n'est-ce pas?*	
13.	*Oui. Il ne joue pas.*	
14.	*Est-ce qu'il ne joue plus?*	
15.	*Oh, il joue encore. Il joue souvent.*	
16.	*Il va jouer ce soir.*	
17.	*Combien coûte ce concert?*	

PART 3
(20 points—2 points each) Translate the French phrases into English.

18.	*Elle avançait très lentement.*	
19.	*Mais elle ne s'est pas arrêtée.*	
20.	*Elle n'a pas abandonné.*	
21.	*Je sois si fatiguée.*	
22.	*Je ne peux pas m'arrêter.*	
23.	*Je dois aller de l'avant.*	
24.	*Il ne savait pas combien de temps il avait dormi.*	
25.	*Il a regardé en arrière, mais il n'a pas vu la tortue.*	
26.	*La tortue a gagné.*	
27.	*Et tous les animaux ont applaudi.*	

PART 4
(20 points—2 points each) Translate the following phrases into either English or French, according to the space provided.

28.	And how is your husband?	
29.		*Bien, tout va bien chez nous.*
30.	How are you doing? Everything OK?	
31.		*Je ne t'ai pas vu depuis longtemps.*
32.	I have not seen you since fall.	
33.		*Et c'est déjà 1999.*
34.	By the way, happy new year.	
35.		*Pour toi aussi.*
36.	Are you coming from work?	
37.		*Non, d'une leçon de chant.*

PART 5—LISTENING COMPREHENSION
(26 points—2 points each) Listen to the following story about an artist who wants to paint the most beautiful thing in the world. As he searches to discover how to paint it, he meets four people on the road who each have different opinions on what the most beautiful thing in the world is. Fill in the chart below based on the story. The story will be repeated twice on the audio.

Person	Their opinion	How the artist depicts that quality
38.	39.	40.
41.	42.	43.
44.	45.	46.
47.	48.	49.

50. What does the artist paint for the most beautiful thing in the world?

French Test 11

Name _____
Total _____/100 points

PART 1
(20 points—2 points each) Translate the English phrases into French.

1.	There were once three pigs.	
2.	Three little pigs.	
3.	They were brothers.	
4.	But they had different characters.	
5.	One day they were talking.	
6.	They wanted to build a house.	
7.	As they were talking they saw a man in a truck with a load of straw.	
8.	Let's build a house of straw.	
9.	No, we don't want a house of straw.	
10.	Well, then, I am going to build it myself.	

PART 2
(20 points—2 points each) Match the French phrase with the English translation.

11.	*Voici maintenant mon histoire.*	
12.	*D'abord la femme prépare la nourriture.*	
13.	*Voici la femme préparant la nourriture.*	
14.	*Après cela la souris vient et mange la nourriture.*	
15.	*Voici la souris mangeant la nourriture.*	
16.	*Après cela le chat vient et attrape la souris.*	
17.	*Voici le serpent avalant le chat.*	

18.	*Après cela l'aigle vient et avale le chat.*	
19.	*Voici l'aigle s'abattant sur le serpent.*	
20.	*Après cela l'aigle vient et s'abat sur le serpent.*	

PART 3

(20 points—2 points each) Translate the French phrases into English.

21.	____	*Tout ce qui brille n'est pas d'or.*	a.	All that glitters is not gold.
22.	____	*Tout est bien qui finit bien.*	b.	Better late than never.
23.	____	*Mieux vaut tard que jamais.*	c.	All's well that ends well.
24.	____	*Qui se ressemble s'assemble.*	d.	Man proposes but God disposes.
25.	____	*Rira bien qui rira le dernier.*	e.	Birds of a feather flock together.
26.	____	*Aide-toi, le ciel t'aidera.*	f.	He who laughs last laughs best.
27.	____	*L'homme propose mais Dieu dispose.*	g.	Nothing ventured, nothing gained.
28.	____	*Point de nouvelles, bonnes nouvelles.*	h.	No news is good news.
29.	____	*Qui ne risque rien, n'a rien.*	i.	Heaven helps those who help themselves.
30.	____	*On ne doit pas dire du mal de ses voisins.*	j.	One shouldn't speak ill of one's neighbors.

PART 4

(10 points) Match the English word with the French equivalent.

31.	____	sky	a.	*la mer*
32.	____	cloud	b.	*le temps*
33.	____	sun	c.	*la lune*
34.	____	moon	d.	*la pluie*
35.	____	stars	e.	*le ciel*
36.	____	sea	f.	*les étoiles*
37.	____	storm	g.	*le brouillard*
38.	____	fog	h.	*l'orage*
39.	____	rain	i.	*le nuage*
40.	____	weather	j.	*le soleil*

PART 5—LISTENING COMPREHENSION

(30 points—2 points each) Read the following questions that are based on the story "The Hermit and the Three Robbers." Listen to the story on the audio. Answer the questions (in English) based on what you hear. The story will be repeated twice on the audio.

41. Where does the hermit live?

42. Why does he become a hermit?

43. What is the weather like when the story takes place?

44. What does he see in the back of the cave?

45. What happens as he is running from the cave?

46. What two things does he tell the robbers he is fleeing from?

47. Does the hermit ever tell the robbers what the evil is?

48. After returning to the cave, what does the hermit warn will happen to the robbers if they don't flee?

49. What three things is the youngest robber supposed to buy in the village?

50. What happens to the hermit after he has shown the robbers the cave?

51. What plan does the young robber make while going to the village?

52. What plan do the two older thieves make?

53. How does the younger robber die?

54. What happens to the other two robbers?

55. Is the hermit's prophesy fulfilled?

French Test 12

Name _____
Total _____ /100 points

PART 1
(10 points—2 points each) Translate the English phrases into French.

1.	Have you ever seen a giant?	
2.	Do you know how big a giant is?	
3.	Do you know how much a hungry giant can eat?	
4.	I don't like spiders.	
5.	He ran home as fast he could.	

PART 2
(20 points—2 points each) Translate the French phrases into English.

6.	*Dans une maison, d'un côté du bois vit une petite fille avec sa mère et son père.*	
7.	*Elle s'appelle Le Petit Chaperon Rouge.*	
8.	*Sa grand-mère habite de l'autre côté du bois.*	
9.	*Ta grand-mère est malade.*	
10.	*Apporte-lui ce panier de biscuits.*	
11.	*Oui maman, avec plaisir.*	
12.	*Mais fais attention, ma chérie.*	
13.	*Ne parle avec personne.*	
14.	*On dit qu'il y a un loup féroce dans le bois.*	
15.	*J'ai faim.*	

Part 3

(20 points—2 points each) Translate the French phrases into English.

16.	*Oh oui, je la connais.*	
17.	*Es-tu le loup?*	
18.	*Oui, mais n'aie pas peur.*	
19.	*J'aime les petites filles.*	
20.	*Quel est ton nom?*	
21.	*Eh bien, je dois m'en aller.*	
22.	*Le Petit Chaperon Rouge continue son chemin en sifflant.*	
23.	*Il frappe à la porte.*	
24.	*Le loup imite la voix de la petite fille.*	
25.	*Grand-mère sort rapidement du lit et sort en courant de la maison.*	

Part 4

(20 points—2 points each) Translate the French phrases into English.

26.	*Il était une fois un jeune homme qui voulait peindre la plus belle chose au monde.*	
27.	*Ne sachant pas où elle était ni où la trouver, il quitta sa famille et partit parcourir le monde à sa recherche.*	
28.	*La foi est certainement la plus belle chose au monde.*	
29.	*C'est facile.*	
30.	*Et autour de sa maison il vit la paix.*	
31.	*Comme vous avez l'air heureuse!*	
32.	*Vous avez vécu près de la nature.*	
33.	*C'est très simple.*	

| 34. | *Dans les yeux de ses enfants il vit l'espoir.* | |
| 35. | *N'oublions pas que dans nos propres foyers nous trouvons la foi, l'espoir, l'amour et la paix.* | |

PART 5—LISTENING COMPREHENSION

(30 points) Listen to the story "Maliang and the Magic Brush." In English, write everything that you understand. As you listen to the story a second time, make your notes more complete.

French Test 10 Answers

PART 1 (14 POINTS)
1. *Je comprends ça.* 2. *Mais maintenant mon père est en colère contre moi.* 3. *C'est la vie.* 4. *Cherches-tu du travail?* 5. *Où travailles-tu maintenant?* 6. *A la librairie.* 7. *Comment s'appelle-t-elle?*

PART 2 (20 POINTS)
8. Who is singing? 9. The king. The king is singing. 10. Which king? 11. Bobi and Misti are singing too. 12. The king that loves to play the drum is singing now, right? 13. Yes. He is not playing. 14. Doesn't he play anymore? 15. Oh, he still plays. He often plays. 16. He's going to play tonight. 17. How much does this concert cost?

PART 3 (20 POINTS)
18. She moved very slowly. 19. But she didn't stop herself. 20. She didn't give up. 21. I am so tired. 22. I cannot stop myself. 23. I must press on. 24. He didn't know how long he'd been sleeping. 25. He looked back but he didn't see the tortoise. 26. The tortoise won. 27. And all the animals cheered.

PART 4 (20 POINTS)
28. *Et comment va ton mari?* 29. Fine, everything is fine with us. 30. *Comment vas-tu? Tout va bien?* 31. I have not seen you for a long time. 32. *Je ne t'ai pas vue depuis l'automne.* 33. And it's already 1999. 34. *Au fait, bonne année.* 35. Same to you. 36. *Tu reviens du travail?* 37. No, from a singing lesson.

PART 5 (26 POINTS)
38. Priest 39. Faith 40. The forehead of his mother 41. Farmer 42. Hope 43. Eyes of his children 44. Bride 45. Love 46. Smile of his wife 47. Wounded soldier 48. Peace 49. Around his house 50. His home and family

French Test 11 Answers

PART 1 (20 POINTS)
1. *Il était une fois trois cochons.* 2. *Trois petits cochons.* 3. *Ils étaient frères.* 4. *Mais ils avaient des caractères différents.* 5. *Un jour, ils parlaient.* 6. *Ils voulaient construire une maison.* 7. *Pendant qu'ils parlaient ils ont vu un homme dans un camion avec un chargement de paille.* 8. *Construisons une maison en paille.* 9. *Non nous ne voulons pas de maison en paille.* 10. *Bon alors, je la construirai moi-même.*

PART 2 (20 POINTS)
11. Here now is my story. 12. At first the woman prepares the food. 13. Here's the woman preparing the food. 14. After this the mouse comes and eats the food. 15. Here's the mouse eating the food. 16. After this the cat comes and catches the mouse. 17. Here's the snake swallowing the cat. 18. After this the eagle comes and swallows the cat. 19. Here's the eagle pouncing on the snake. 20. After this the eagle comes and pounces on the snake.

PART 3 (20 POINTS)
21. a. 22. c. 23. b. 24. e. 25. f. 26. i. 27. d. 28. h. 29. g. 30. j.

PART 4 (10 POINTS)
31. e 32. i 33. j 34. c 35. f 36. a 37. h 38. g 39. d 40. b

PART 5 (30 POINTS)
41. In the mountains. 42. Because he was revolted by materialism in the world. 43. It's raining. 44. Gold 45. He is stopped by three thieves. 46. Evil and death. 47. No. 48. They will die. 49. A cart, wine, and meat. 50. He leaves. 51. He decided to poison the other two thieves so he can have more money. 52. They plan to kill the younger thief when he returns so they can have more money. 53. He is stabbed. 54. They die from the poison. 55. Yes.

French Test 12 Answers

PART 1 (10 POINTS)
1. *As-tu déjà vu un géant?* 2. *Sais-tu combien mesure un géant?* 3. *Sais-tu combien un géant affamé peut manger?* 4. *Je n'aime pas les araignées.* 5. *Il est rentré chez lui en courant aussi vite qu'il pouvait.*

PART 2 (20 POINTS)
6. In a house on one side of the woods there lives a little girl with her mother and her father. 7. She's called Little Red Riding Hood. 8. Her grandmother lives on the other side of the woods. 9. Your grandmother is sick. 10. Take her this basket of cookies. 11. Yes, Mother, with pleasure. 12. But be careful, dear. 13. Don't talk to anyone. 14. They say that there's a ferocious wolf in the woods. 15. I am hungry.

PART 3 (20 POINTS)
16. Oh yes, I know her. 17. Are you the wolf? 18. Yes, but you needn't fear. 19. I love little girls. 20. What is your name? 21. Well then, I have to go now. 22. Red Riding Hood continues on her way, whistling. 23. He knocks on the door. 24. The wolf imitates the little girl's voice. 25. Grand-mother quickly gets out of bed and runs out of the house.

PART 4 (20 POINTS)
26. Once there was a young man who wanted to paint the most beautiful thing in the world. 27. Not knowing what it was or where to find it, he left his family and went out into the world to search for it. 28. Surely faith is the most beautiful thing in the world. 29. That is very easy. 30. And around his house he saw peace. 31. How happy you look! 32. You have lived close to nature. 33. That is very simple. 34. In the eyes of his children he saw hope. 35. Let us not forget that in our own home we find faith, hope, love, and peace.

PART 5 (30 POINTS)
This question type is called a recall protocol. To grade it, read what the examinee has written and compare it to the story. Assign the examinee a score based on the completeness and correctness of the answer. The story is entitled "Maliang and the Magic Brush." It is found in the "Transcripts" section.

French Test 10 Transcript

THE MOST BEAUTIFUL THING IN THE WORLD
La plus belle chose au monde

Once there was a young artist who wanted to paint the most beautiful thing in the world.	*Il était une fois un jeune artiste qui voulait peindre la plus belle chose au monde.*
Not knowing what it was or where to find it, he left his family and went out into the world to search for it.	*Ne sachant pas où elle était ni où la trouver, il quitta sa famille et partit parcourir le monde à sa recherche.*
As he traveled about, he saw an old priest. He said to him: "Father, you have lived very long and you look wise. Can you tell me what the most beautiful thing in the world is?"	*En voyageant, il vit un vieux prêtre. Il lui dit: «Père, vous avez vécu très longtemps et vous avez l'air très sage. Pouvez-vous me dire ce qu'est la plus belle chose au monde?»*
The old priest replied: "That is very simple: surely faith is the most beautiful thing in the world."	*Le vieux prêtre répondit: «C'est très simple: la foi est certainement la plus belle chose au monde.»*
Pondering the priest's answer, but unsure how to paint faith, the young artist traveled on until he came to an old farmer.	*Réfléchissant à la réponse du prêtre, mais ne sachant pas comment peindre la foi, le jeune artiste continua à voyager jusqu'à ce qu'il rencontra un vieux fermier.*
"Kind sir," he said to the farmer, "you have lived close to nature. Can you tell me what the most beautiful thing in the world is?"	*«Bon monsieur», dit-il au fermier, «vous avez vécu près de la nature. Pouvez-vous me dire ce qui est la plus belle chose au monde?»*
The farmer replied: "That is easy: surely hope is the most beautiful thing in the world."	*Le fermier répondit: «C'est facile: l'espoir est certainement la plus belle chose au monde.»*
Pondering the answers of the farmer and the priest, yet not knowing how he could depict faith and hope, the artist traveled on until he came to a young bride.	*Réfléchissant aux réponses du fermier et du prêtre, et ne sachant toujours pas comment dépeindre la foi et l'espoir, l'artiste continua à voyager jusqu'à rencontrer une jeune mariée.*
He said to her: "How happy you look! Can you tell me what the most beautiful thing in the world is?"	*Il lui dit: «Comme vous avez l'air heureuse! Pouvez-vous me dire qu'elle est la plus belle chose au monde?»*
The bride replied: "That is easy: surely love is the most beautiful thing in the world."	*La mariée répondit: «C'est facile: l'amour est certainement la plus belle chose au monde.»*
Not knowing how he could depict love, the artist traveled on until he came to a wounded soldier limping home from war.	*Ne sachant pas comment dépeindre l'amour, l'artiste continua à voyager jusqu'à rencontrer un soldat blessé rentrant de la guerre chez lui en boitant.*
He asked him: "Can you tell me what the most beautiful thing in the world is?"	*Il lui demanda: «Peux-tu me dire quelle est la plus belle chose au monde?»*
The soldier replied: "That is easy: surely peace is the most beautiful thing in the world."	*Le soldat répondit: «C'est facile: la paix est certainement la plus belle chose au monde.»*
The young artist pondered what the priest, the farmer, the bride, and the soldier had said, but thought:	*Le jeune artiste réfléchit à ce que le prêtre, le fermier, la mariée, et le soldat avaient dit, mais pensa:*
How can I depict faith, hope, love, and peace in one picture?	*Comment puis-je dépeindre la foi, l'espoir, l'amour, et la paix en une seule image?*
Thinking there was nothing further he could learn, he turned back and returned home.	*Pensant qu'il ne pouvait pas en apprendre davantage, il fit demi-tour et rentra chez lui.*
The moment he entered his home, he saw the following:	*Au moment où il entra chez lui, il vit la chose suivante:*
In the forehead of his mother he saw faith.	*Sur le front de sa mère il vit la foi.*

In the eyes of his children he saw hope.	*Dans les yeux de ses enfants il vit l'espoir.*
In the smile of his wife he saw love.	*Dans le sourire de sa femme il vit l'amour.*
And around his house he saw peace.	*Et autour de sa maison il vit la paix.*
At once the young artist set about to paint the picture of the most beautiful thing in the world.	*Aussitôt le jeune artiste se mit à peindre la plus belle chose au monde.*
And that picture was nothing more than his own home and family.	*Et ce tableau n'était rien de plus que sa propre maison et sa famille.*
Let us not forget that in our own home we find faith, hope, love, and peace,	*N'oublions pas que dans nos propres foyers nous trouvons la foi, l'espoir, l'amour, et la paix,*
and these are surely the most beautiful things in the world.	*et ce sont certainement les choses les plus belles au monde.*

French Test 11 Transcript

THE HERMIT AND THE THREE ROBBERS
L'ermite et les trois voleurs

(A Medieval Tale from Italy)	*(Un conte médiéval d'Italie)*
There was once a hermit who lived in the mountains.	*Il était une fois un ermite qui vivait dans les montagnes.*
Revolted by the materialism that dominated the hearts of men he had turned to a life of contemplation.	*Révolté par le matérialisme qui dominait le coeur des hommes, il s'était tourné vers une vie de contemplation.*
One day as he was walking through the forest, a storm came up.	*Un jour comme il marchait dans la forêt, un orage éclata.*
Seeing a space between two large boulders, he sought shelter there.	*Voyant un espace entre deux grands rochers, il s'y mit à l'abri.*
Once under the shelter of the rocks, he noticed a narrow opening in the side of the mountain.	*Une fois à l'abri des rochers, il remarqua une ouverture étroite sur le côté de la montagne.*
Curious, he crawled into the opening and discovered a large cave.	*Curieux, il rampa dans l'ouverture et découvrit une grande grotte.*
As his eyes grew accustomed to the dark inside the cave, he noticed something shining at the back.	*Quand ses yeux s'habituèrent à l'obscurité de l'intérieur de la grotte, il remarqua quelque chose de brillant au fond.*
It turned out to be a heap of gold.	*Cela s'avéra être un tas d'or.*
Quickly he turned and crawled out and fled in terror through the forest in spite of the rain.	*Il fit vite demi-tour et sortit en rampant et s'enfuit terrorisé à travers la forêt malgré la pluie.*
As he was running, he came upon three robbers.	*Comme il courait, il rencontra trois voleurs.*
Wondering what he was running from, they stopped him and asked: "Why are you running through the rain? Is the devil in pursuit of you?"	*Se demandant ce qu'il fuyait, ils l'arrêtèrent et demandèrent: «Pourquoi cours-tu sous cette pluie? Est-ce que le diable est à ta poursuite?»*
"No. It is not the devil chasing me. I am running from evil."	*«Non. Ce n'est pas le diable qui me poursuit. Je fuis le mal.»*
"What evil inspires you to run like this through the rain?"	*«Quel mal te fait donc courir comme cela sous la pluie?»*
"Don't ask to know. It would destroy any man. It would destroy you."	*«Ne cherchez pas à savoir. Cela détruirait n'importe quel homme. Cela vous détruirait.»*
Hearing this, the robbers became very curious.	*En entendant cela, les voleurs devinrent très curieux.*

"Tell us," they said, "what is the nature of the evil that threatens you?"	«Dis-nous» dirent-ils, «de quelle nature est le mal qui te menace?»
"I dare not even speak of it," said the hermit.	«Je n'ose même pas en parler» dit l'ermite.
"You must tell us. We're not afraid."	«Tu dois nous dire. Nous n'avons pas peur.»
"No, I cannot. I must not."	«Non, je ne peux pas. Je ne dois pas.»
"You will tell us or we will kill you! Come, lead us to it."	«Tu nous le dis ou nous te tuons! Viens, conduis-nous y.»
"I am running from Death. He is close behind. Flee with me, I beg you."	«Je fuis la Mort. Elle est juste derrière. Fuyez avec moi, je vous en prie.»
"You are insane. No one is pursuing you. Come, lead us to Death. Show us what it is you fear."	«Tu es fou. Personne ne te poursuit. Viens, conduis-nous vers la Mort. Montre-nous ce qui te fait peur.»
The poor hermit was terrified. He took them to the mouth of the cave, but warned them, saying: "I warn you, do not enter this dangerous place.	Le pauvre ermite était terrifié. Il les amena à l'entrée de la grotte, mais les avertit, disant: «Je vous avertis, n'entrez pas dans cet endroit dangereux.
Flee before it is too late. Your lives are in jeopardy."	Fuyez avant qu'il ne soit trop tard. Vos vies sont en danger.»
Dragging him by the hand, the robbers crawled through the narrow opening into the cave, and there they found the gold.	Le traînant par la main, les voleurs se glissèrent à l'intérieur de la grotte par l'étroite ouverture, et là ils trouvèrent l'or.
"Here is Death," said the hermit. "If you give in to his clutches, he will kill you."	«Voici la Mort» dit l'ermite. «Si vous vous abandonnez dans ses griffes, elle vous tuera.»
Laughing greedily, the robbers began to assess their treasure.	Riant avec avarice, les voleurs commencèrent à s'approprier le trésor.
"It is too heavy to carry.	«Il est trop lourd à porter.
One of us must go to the village and secure a cart."	L'un de nous doit aller au village et ramener une charette.»
"Yes, and bring meat and wine so we can celebrate our good fortune."	«Oui, et ramener de la viande et du vin afin que nous célébrions notre bonne fortune.»
Laughing at the hermit's absurd fear, they sent him on his way, warning him never to come back, lest death overtake him.	Riant de la peur absurde de l'ermite, ils le renvoyèrent, l'avertissant de ne jamais revenir, à moins que la mort ne l'enlève.
Furthermore, they told him, if he ever spoke a word about this, for sure he would be killed.	En outre, ils lui dirent que si jamais il disait un mot à ce sujet, il serait sûrement tué.
Then the two older ones sent the younger one off to the village with a gold coin to bring a cart and some meat and wine.	Puis les deux plus âgés envoyèrent le plus jeune au village avec quelques pièces d'or pour ramener une charette, de la viande et du vin.
As he was walking to the village, he thought up a plan.	Comme il marchait vers le village il pensa à un plan.
"Even dividing the fortune three ways the three of us are enormously rich.	«Même en divisant la fortune en trois, nous serons tous les trois énormément riches.
But if it were not divided, if it all fell to me, I would be the richest man in Italy.	Mais si elle n'était pas divisée, si elle me revenait toute, je serais l'homme le plus riche d'Italie.
My companions have not always dealt fairly with me.	Mes compagnons n'ont pas toujours été justes avec moi.
Now we'll have a settlement of accounts.	Maintenant nous allons avoir un règlement de comptes.
I will pay them back what they deserve, then I'll be the sole master of the treasure."	Je leur donnerai ce qu'ils méritent, et ensuite je serai le seul maître du trésor.»
In the village he quickly found what he was seeking.	Dans le village il trouva vite ce qu'il cherchait.

With the gold, he rented a cart and bought a good supply of meat and wine, and also a small vial of poison.	*Avec l'or, il loua une charette à bras et acheta une bonne provision de viande et de vin, et aussi une petite fiole de poison.*
He poured the poison into the wine.	*Il versa le poison dans le vin.*
"Ha!" he said to himself. "When my companions drink the wine, they'll die, and the treasure will be mine alone."	*«Ha!» se dit-il. «Quand mes compagnons boiront le vin, ils mourront, et le trésor sera pour moi tout seul.»*
The two robbers waiting in the cave, gloating over their new-found treasure while their companion was absent, thought up a scheme of their own.	*Les deux voleurs qui attendaient dans la grotte, et qui jubilaient à la vue de leur nouveau trésor pendant que leur compagnon était absent, établirent aussi leur plan.*
"A sharing of the treasure by two persons would yield to each considerably more among three.	*«Un partage en deux rapporterait à chacun considérablement plus qu'un partage en trois.*
We have only to do away with our companion and we each gain very much for ourselves."	*Il nous suffit de nous débarrasser de notre compagnon et nous gagnerons beaucoup pour nous-mêmes.»*
So when their companion arrived with the cart and the food and wine, these two fell upon him with knives.	*Alors, quand leur compagnon est arrivé avec la charette à bras, la nourriture et le vin, ces deux-là lui sont tombés des surs lui avec des couteaux.*
Then they feasted upon the provisions he had brought.	*Ensuite, ils ont fait la fête avec les provisions qu'il avait apportées.*
Before long, they were seized with violent pangs, and as they lay dying, they thought of the hermit's dire warning:	*Après peu de temps, ils ont été saisis de violents battements de cœur et alors qu'ils étaient étendus prêts à mourir, ils ont pensé aux terribles avertissements de l'ermite:*
"I tell you, do not enter this cursèd place.	*«Je vous le dis, n'entrez pas dans cet endroit maudit.*
Flee before it is too late. Your lives are in jeopardy."	*Enfuyez-vous avant qu'il ne soit trop tard. Vos vies sont en danger.»*
To this day, no one has taken the gold from the cave.	*Jusqu'à présent, personne n'a pris l'or de la cave.*
How about you? If you knew where to find it, would you dare take it?	*Et vous? Si vous saviez où le trouver, oseriez-vous le prendre?*

French Test 12 Transcript

MALIANG AND THE MAGIC BRUSH
Maliang et le pinceau magique

Once there was a boy named Maliang.	*Il était une fois un garçon qui s'appelait Maliang.*
Since the time he was small he liked to draw but his family was too poor to have even a brush.	*Depuis qu'il était petit, il aimait peindre mais sa famille était trop pauvre pour avoir même un seul pinceau.*
One day as he was herding cows home, he passed by a school and saw a painter inside painting a picture for a magistrate.	*Un jour, alors qu'il ramenait des vaches à la maison, il est passé près d'une école et a vu un peintre qui peignait à l'intérieur pour un magistrat.*
The magistrate and his attendants were by his side watching.	*Ce magistrat et ses assistants observaient à ses côtés.*
Maliang was so fascinated that without stopping to think he went in.	*Maliang était si fasciné qu'il est entré sans réfléchir.*
He said to the magistrate and the painter: "Could you let me use one of your brushes? I'd like to learn to draw."	*Il a dit au magistrat et au peintre: «Pourriez-vous me laisser utiliser vos pinceaux? Je voudrais apprendre à peindre.»*
Hearing this the magistrate and teacher roared with laughter, and said: "A poor boy wants to learn to draw too?"	*En entendant cela, le magistrat et le professeur ont éclaté de rire, et ils ont dit: «Un garçon pauvre veut aussi apprendre à peindre?»*
Maliang said: "Well, I think a poor boy could learn to draw."	*Maliang a dit: «Eh bien, je pense qu'un garçon pauvre peut apprendre à peindre.»*
After that incident, Maliang practiced drawing with heart and soul.	*Après cet incident, Maliang s'est mis à s'exercer de tout son cœur et de toute son âme.*
When he went into the hills to gather wood, he would use a stick to draw birds in the sky.	*Quand il allait dans les collines pour ramasser du bois, il utilisait un bâton pour peindre des oiseaux dans le ciel.*
When he went to the riverside to cut straw, he'd use his finger to draw fish in the sand.	*Quand il allait à la rivière pour couper de la paille, il utilisait son doigt pour peindre des poissons dans le sable.*
Whatever he saw, he would draw.	*Il pouvait peindre tout ce qu'il voyait.*
A person asked him: "Maliang, when you've learned to draw will you go and draw for the magistrates?"	*Une personne lui a demandé: «Maliang, quand tu auras appris à dessiner, iras-tu peindre pour les magistrats?»*
Maliang shook his head and said: "No. Never! I'll only draw for the poor."	*Maliang a secoué sa tête et a dit: «Non. Jamais! Je ne peindrai que pour les pauvres.»*
The days went by and Maliang progressed rapidly in his talent.	*Les jours passaient et Maliang progressait rapidement dans son talent.*
But he still had no brush.	*Mais il n'avait toujours pas de pinceau.*
How he longed to have a brush! One night he was lying in bed.	*Comme il désirait avoir un pinceau! Une nuit, il était couché dans son lit.*
All of a sudden a golden shaft of light illuminated the room.	*Tout à coup, un rayon doré de lumière a illuminé la chambre.*
An old man with a white beard appeared before him.	*Un vieil homme avec une barbe blanche lui est apparu.*

The old man handed him a brush and said: "Maliang, now that you have a brush remember your own words: draw only for the poor."	Le vieil homme lui a tendu un pinceau et a dit: «Maliang, maintenant que tu as un pinceau, souviens-toi de tes propres paroles: ne peins que pour les pauvres.»
Maliang was truly happy.	Maliang était vraiment heureux.
He immediately took the brush and drew a rooster on the wall.	Il a immédiatement pris le pinceau et a dessiné un coq sur le mur.
Miraculously, the rooster came alive, flew down from the wall, jumped onto the window sill and began to crow.	Par miracle, le coq est devenu vivant, s'est envolé du mur, a sauté sur le bord de la fenêtre et s'est mis à faire cocorico.
It turned out that the brush the old man gave him was magic.	Il s'est révélé que le pinceau que le vieil homme lui avait donné était magique.
With this magic brush, every day Maliang drew pictures for the poor people.	Avec ce pinceau magique, Maliang a dessiné des images pour les pauvres chaque jour.
Whatever they wanted he would draw.	Il leur peignait tout ce qu'ils voulaient.
Whatever he drew they would have.	Ils obtenaient tout ce qu'il dessinait.
One day while he was passing by a field, he saw a farmer and his child pulling a plow to till the soil.	Un jour, alors qu'il passait près d'un champ, il a vu un fermier et son fils qui tiraient une charrue pour labourer le sol.
The ground was so hard they could barely move the plow.	Le sol était si dur qu'ils pouvaient à peine bouger la charrue.
Maliang took his magic brush out and drew a big ox for them.	Maliang a sorti son pinceau magique et leur a dessiné un grand bœuf.
"Moo." The ox went to work plowing.	«Meuh.» Le bœuf se mit à travailler, à labourer la terre.
A magistrate heard Maliang had a magic brush and sent his soldiers to fetch him and bring him to the court.	Un magistrat a entendu que Maliang avait un pinceau magique et lui a envoyé ses soldats pour aller le chercher et l'emmener à la cour.
He wanted him to draw some gold bricks.	Il voulait qu'il peigne quelques lingots d'or.
Maliang hated the magistrate. Standing motionless, he cried out: "I can't paint."	Maliang détestait le magistrat. Se tenant debout sans bouger, il a crié: «Je ne sais pas peindre.»
The magistrate got extremely angry and locked him in prison.	Le magistrat s'est fâché à l'extrême et l'a enfermé en prison.
When midnight came, the guard fell fast asleep.	A minuit, le garde s'est endormi.
Maliang, with his magic brush, drew a door on the wall, and when he gave it a push it opened.	Maliang, avec son pinceau magique, a dessiné une porte sur le mur et quand il l'a poussée, elle s'est ouverte.
He said: "Fellow villagers, let's get out of here."	Il a dit: «Concitoyens, partons d'ici.»
All the poor prisoners followed him and escaped.	Tous les pauvres prisonniers l'ont suivi et se sont échappés.
When the magistrate heard that Maliang had escaped he sent his soldiers to catch him.	Quand le magistrat a entendu que Maliang s'était échappé, il a envoyé ses soldats pour l'attraper.
But earlier Maliang had drawn a fast horse.	Mais auparavant, Maliang avait peint un cheval rapide.
He mounted the horse and rode far off where they could not catch up with him.	Il est monté sur le cheval et est parti très loin où ils ne pouvaient pas le rattraper.
One day he arrived at a place where the ground was parched.	Un jour, il est arrivé à un endroit où le sol était desséché.

The peasants had no water wheel so they had to carry water in buckets.	Les paysans n'avaient pas de roue hydraulique et ils devaient donc porter les seaux d'eau.
"Hang yow, hang yow," they chanted as they strained.	Ils chantaient: «Oh hisse! Oh hisse!» alors qu'ils faisaient de gros efforts.
Maliang said: "Let me draw you some water wheels."	Maliang a dit: «Laissez-moi vous peindre quelques roues hydrauliques.»
Getting water wheels, the peasants were happy.	Les paysans étaient heureux de recevoir des roues hydrauliques.
Just then, several guards stepped out of the crowd, put chains around Maliang's neck, and took him away.	A ce moment précis, quelques gardes sont sortis de la foule ont mis des chaînes au cou de Maliang, et l'ont emporté.
The magistrate, seated in the great court, shouted repeatedly: "Take Maliang and tie him up. Take his brush away from him and send at once for the painter."	Le magistrat, assis à la grande cour, criait sans arrêt: «Saisissez-vous de Maliang et enchaînez-le. Prenez-lui son pinceau et appelez tout de suite un peintre.»
When the painter came the magistrate asked him to draw a precious coin tree.	Quand le peintre est arrivé, le magistrat lui a demandé de lui peindre un arbre à monnaies précieuses.
The painter took Maliang's brush and painted a precious coin tree.	Le peintre a pris le pinceau de Maliang et a peint un arbre à monnaies précieuses.
The magistrate was overjoyed.	Le magistrat était fou de joie.
He ran hastily to the tree but only hit his head on the wall, giving himself a bruise on his forehead.	Il a couru très vite vers l'arbre mais n'a fait que se cogner la tête contre le mur, ce qui lui a donné un bleu sur le front.
The painting was still a painting. It had not turned into a real precious coin tree.	Le dessin était toujours un dessin. Il ne s'était pas transformé en un vrai arbre à monnaies précieuses.
The magistrate came over to Maliang, untied him and in a voice that feigned sweetness, said: "Maliang, good Maliang, wouldn't you draw a nice picture for me?"	Le magistrat s'est approché de Maliang, l'a détaché et, en feignant une voix douce, et a dit: «Maliang, mon bon Maliang, ne peindras-tu pas un beau dessin pour moi?»
Intending to get his magic brush back, Maliang replied: "All right. I'll draw you a picture one time."	Avec l'intention de récupérer son pinceau magique, Maliang a répondu: «D'accord. Je te peindrai un dessin une seule fois.»
The magistrate, seeing Maliang agree, took the magic brush and gave it back, asking him to draw a gold mountain.	Le magistrat, voyant que Maliang était d'accord, prit le pinceau magique et le lui rendit en lui demandant de peindre une montagne d'or.
Maliang didn't say anything, but on the wall with his magic brush he drew a sea with no end.	Maliang n'a rien dit, mais, sur le mur, avec son pinceau magique, il a peint une mer sans fin.
The magistrate furiously said: "Who asked you to draw a sea?	Le magistrat a dit avec fureur: «Qui t'a demandé de peindre une mer?
Draw me a gold mountain...Now!"	Peins-moi une montagne d'or...Maintenant!»
Maliang made some strokes with his brush.	Maliang a donné quelques coups de pinceau.
In the middle of the sea a gold mountain appeared.	Au milieu de la mer, il est apparu une montagne d'or.
A mountain of glittering gold.	Une montagne d'or brillant.
The magistrate jumped straight up and said over and over: "Quick, draw a big boat--draw a big boat. I want to climb the gold mountain and carry off the gold."	Le magistrat a sauté en l'air et a dit encore et encore: «Vite, peins un grand bateau--peins un grand bateau. Je veux escalader la montagne et en emporter l'or.»
Maliang drew a big boat.	Maliang a peint un grand bateau.

Taking his soldiers, the magistrate jumped on board and said: "Quick, set sail, set sail!"	*Le magistrat a sauté sur le bateau en emportant ses soldats et a dit: «Vite, mettez les voiles, mettez les voiles.»*
Maliang drew some gusts of wind and the sails picked it up.	*Maliang a peint quelques bourrasques de vent et les voiles se sont gonflées.*
The boat started sailing out to the sea.	*Le bateau se mit à naviguer en direction de la mer.*
The magistrate thought the boat was too slow.	*Le magistrat a pensé que le bateau était trop lent.*
So, standing on the bow, he shouted: "More wind! More wind!"	*Alors, debout dans le bateau, il a crié: «Plus de vent, plus de vent!»*
Again Maliang drew several fierce gusts of wind.	*A nouveau, Maliang a peint quelques bourrasques de vent violentes.*
The sea's waters became rough and the boat began to rock.	*Les eaux de la mer sont devenues houleuses et le bateau se mit à tanguer.*
The magistrate became frightened and said, begging for mercy: "Enough wind, enough wind!"	*Le magistrat a pris peur et a dit, implorant la pitié: «Assez de vent, assez de vent!»*
But Maliang paid no attention to him and continued to draw more wind.	*Mais Maliang n'a pas fait attention à lui et a continué à peindre davantage de vent.*
The wind got still fiercer and the sea began to roar.	*Le vent est devenu encore plus violent et la mer se mit à rugir.*
Finally the waters became like mountains striking against the boat.	*A la fin, les eaux sont devenues comme des montagnes, s'abattant sur le bateau.*
The boat capsized.	*Le bateau s'est retourné.*
The magistrate and all the others sank to the bottom of the sea.	*Le magistrat et tous les autres ont coulé au fond de la mer.*
Maliang went back to the poor people, drawing whatever thing they needed.	*Maliang est retourné vers les pauvres, leur peignant tout ce dont ils avaient besoin.*